Praise for *Joel*

We have known Joel since he first moved to Montreat, North Carolina, eighteen years ago. What an incredible boy he was, what an incredible man he has become—due to the grace of God and his remarkable parents. His strong testimony will stir your heart and forever change you.

RUTH AND BILLY GRAHAM

Joel is a dear friend. His story is truly remarkable. I encourage everyone to read it. It is truly inspiring!

MIKE KRZYZEWSKI, Head Coach, Duke University Basketball

Joel is an American hero. Reading his story will renew your sense of the values many Americans have died for—God, country, and family. True courage is demonstrated in every page.

BOB DOLE, Former United States Senator

The dictionary doesn't have enough adjectives to describe my love and admiration for Joel Sonnenberg. To spend time with Joel—whether in his book, at a soccer game, or over a soda—is to come away a different person, simply because you've been *with* him. When I need perspective on my own pain, I call Joel—he is a priceless treasure in Christ's kingdom.

JONI EARECKSON TADA, Founder and CEO of Joni
and Friends, an international disability ministry

Joel Sonnenberg's story is more than just an uplifting tale of persistence and achievement. Rooted in tragedy, it's the story of a mother's love, a boy's courage, and the resilience of the human spirit. Way to go, Joel!

BRYANT GUMBEL, Television News Journalist

I highly recommend Joel Sonnenberg as a speaker to youth. His story is one all young people need to hear. He has overcome some obstacles but has remained optimistic, confident, and filled with faith. I believe today's youth need to hear stories of people who are truly heroic rather than simply media created.

JAY KESLER, President Emeritus, Taylor University

JOEL SONNENBERG
with GREGG LEWIS

OUACHITA TECHNICAL COLLEGE

ZONDERVAN™

GRAND RAPIDS, MICHIGAN 49530 USA

Z̄ONDERVAN™

Joel
Copyright © 2004 by Joel Sonnenberg

Requests for information should be addressed to:
Zondervan, *Grand Rapids, Michigan 49530*

Library of Congress Cataloging-in-Publication Data

Sonnenberg, Joel.
    Joel / Joel Sonnenberg, with Gregg Lewis.
      p. cm.
    ISBN 0-310-24693-8
    1. Sonnenberg, Joel. 2. Burns and scalds—Patients—United States—Biography.
    3. People with disabilities—United States—Biography. I. Lewis, Gregg, 1951- II. Title.
    RD96.4.S553 2004
    362.197'11'092—dc22
                                                2004003206

This edition printed on acid-free paper.

Published in association with Yates & Yates, LLP, Attorneys and Counselors, Suite 1000, Literary Agent, Orange, CA.

Interior design by Beth Shagene

Printed in the United States of America

---

04 05 06 07 08 09 10 /❖ DC/ 10 9 8 7 6 5

To unique people everywhere,
and to those who are the most special to me—
my parents and family

Acknowledgments

I would like to acknowledge those persons and institutions that significantly contributed to who I am today. The following names are in chronological order:

My Lord and Savior, Jesus Christ

Dad, Mom, Sommer, Kyle, Jami, and Jonathon

Grandma and Grandpa Schneider

Grandma and Grandpa Wilkinson

Aunts, uncles, and cousins

BJ Schnepp

Extended family

Michael Saraceni

Boston Children's Hospital

Shriners Hospitals for Children—Boston and Cincinnati units

Dr. Matt Donelan

Dr. Glen Warden

Betty Dew

Nancy and Alex MacKenzie

Carol Marin

Don Moseley

CAMP-of-the-WOODS

Gordon Purdy

Don and Joanne Purdy

Upper Nyack Elementary administration and teachers

Early childhood friends—Matt, Seth, Griff, Jane Ann, and Peter—and their families

Dr. Sally McGuffey

Leigh Schurholz

Grace Conservative Baptist Church, Nanuet, New York

Dr. Leslie Flynn

The Roger Bosma family

The Dick Norwood family

Ted and Sue Wood

Bob and Gail Hallyburton

The Dr. James Jerele family

The Dr. John Van Wicklin family

Gallimore Elementary administration and teachers

Joyce Darren

Dr. Norma Foster

Darryl Peters

Gerard Damiami

Owen School District (North Carolina)—teachers, administrators, and staff

Ryan Councill

Michael and Judy Councill and family

Montreat Presbyterian Church

The late Dr. Calvin Thielman

Mike and Mickie Krzyzewski

Barrett McFatter

Dr. John Akers

Discover Card—administrators and marketing department

Maury Povich

Rev. Richard and Porsche White

Jordan Berner

Fletcher BMW

Shawn Stewart

Boy Scouts troop 52

Taylor University administration, professors, and staff

Dr. Jay Kesler

Gene Rupp

Walt Campbell

Dr. Dale Jackson

John Aoun

Jeremy Block

All the fellas from First Berg

Bob and Shirley Raese

Michael and Elena Pole and family

Kathy Tarnetzer

Scott Gamel

Jim Flaharty

Jason Martinson

Gregg Lewis

Zondervan team

Check out Joel's website

www.joelsonnenberg.com

Chapter 1

What happened to you? That's the first thought that pops into our minds when we see a person with a cast. If we don't ask it, we at least think it.

I feel like I've lived my whole life wearing a huge, permanent cast with a lot of names written all over it. Everyone who meets me, everyone who sees me, wonders, *What happened to you?*

Rarely a day goes by that I don't hear this question. Some days many times.

Those people who don't come right out and ask still wonder. I can see the question in their eyes and in their reactions—their awkwardness, their silence, their double takes, and their stares. If people don't wonder about me and my story when they meet me, I worry about them. While I try not to take offense if they look at me strange, I definitely look at them strange if they don't.

I can never hide the fact that I'm different. So my response to their *What happened?* question is very often my introduction to people. I've learned that this can be good, or it can be bad—depending on how the story is told. Which is why I began speaking to groups.

Some people act surprised that I'm not too nervous to get up in front of large crowds. In part it's because I know that when I walk into any public situation— whether it's a roomful of twenty partygoers, an auditorium with five thousand people, or a prime-time television show that has millions of viewers—everyone is going to be looking at me anyway. It's only when I'm given the chance to step in front of a microphone or stand up on a stage and share my experience that I have any control over how people look at me or what they think about me. So I actually feel more comfortable in a public-speaking setting where I'm given an opportunity to present myself. It's usually my best chance—sometimes my only chance—to ease the awkwardness, to help people see past the surface so they can understand, or at least accept, me for who I am.

I was not gifted with an incredible athletic talent like Michael Jordan or Tiger Woods. I'm not a musical prodigy who mastered an instrument by the age of six. Nor am I an intellectual genius who learned calculus by kindergarten or graduated from medical school by the age of sixteen. I certainly don't have the imagination or creativity of people like Bill Gates or George Lucas.

There is nothing superhuman about me. I'm just an ordinary person—with an unusual story that in one way or another seems to have an impact on every interaction in my life. Depending on how I choose to respond, this impact can be either positive or negative.

Some mornings I'd much rather sleep in than get up and face the battle of another day. Sometimes I tire of watching and envying people around me who are going through their comfortable daily routine, because what happened to me has determined that my daily life is anything but routine. I have been forced to cope by expecting the unexpected for so long that dealing with surprise has become commonplace for me. I live every day of my life outside the box, consciously trying to change the paradigm, in every interaction with others, to prove that things are not always what they seem. Others' preconceived ideas and false expectations are my constant battleground.

There are occasions when what happened to me becomes a barrier that separates me from other people. But there are also occasions when it has a positive impact on my relationships.

Because many people initially react to me with uncertainty and awkwardness, I'm often forced to tell enough of my story to answer unspoken questions and put people at ease. I've also learned to take the initiative in friendship and to be the first one to speak whenever I meet someone new. In this way I am forced to become more outgoing with others.

Knowing what happened often gives other people an unusual sense of intimacy with me. It makes me seem more transparent and therefore more approachable in many people's minds. I'm constantly humbled by how open and trusting, even vulnerable, many people are when they talk to me. So many hurting people seem to identify with me because of what happened.

We all know that our words, our attitudes, and our actions influence others. But I'm regularly reminded of this when someone comes up to me and says some-

thing like, "Joel, I've never forgotten what you told me that time we were having lunch together at McDonald's. It made such an impact on me." And I'll have
no recollection of what they're talking about. For them it was some life-impacting
conversation; I was just eating a hamburger.

Stuff like that happens to me all the time. When it does, I'm reminded that
what happened to me years ago makes me an example to others.

Not only am I forced to tell my story every day, but any person who has a
relationship with me may be forced to tell it as well. Why? Because other people
ask them, "What happened to Joel?" As a result, in some peculiar way, my story
becomes the story of those around me. Which means it's been told a lot. At least
in part.

I've watched portions of my life reenacted on television. I've read other parts
in newspapers and magazines. I've shared bits and pieces of my personal history
with many acquaintances over the years. I've sat in front of TV cameras and stood
on stage before live audiences to talk about my experience. But this book marks
the first time I've ever told, from my perspective, the whole story of what happened. And I'm excited about the opportunity because I expect new friends,
strangers, and people I've known for years, and even my family, will gain new
insights—not just into my story but also into me. And into life.

C h a p t e r 2

September 15, 1979.

My life changed forever that day. And it took only seconds.

Since I was just twenty-two months old at the time, I have no conscious recollection of what took place that fateful afternoon. I consider that a blessing because I don't know how I would have ever coped with the haunting memories and unforgettably vivid images the other members of my family have endured. For me, the lasting consequences of that autumn Saturday would prove challenge enough. I'll deal with them for the rest of my life.

So I'm thankful I can't remember the events of that day as they happened. But it means I've learned about what happened much like I've studied World History. Like teachers, my parents and others have told me about the day countless times over the years. I've talked to people who were there. I've read many newspaper accounts. I've looked at photos. I've even watched televised reenactments.

I've summarized and retold this part of my story myself time and again in a variety of settings. I know it so well that, as I retell it here, what happened on September 15, 1979, seems every bit as real to me as if I did remember it myself.

Even as a toddler I had sensed the excitement building while my parents packed the car. There hadn't been a real family vacation since my four-year-old sister, Jami, and I were born. So it seemed like a big deal to my folks, Janet and Mike Sonnenberg, to finally be taking this long anticipated weekend trip with my Aunt Kathy and Uncle Doug Rupp from our home in Nyack, New York, to the coast of Maine.

13

Our two-vehicle caravan pulled off at a rest area near the New Hampshire state line so we could all stretch our legs for a few minutes. Jami and I ran around on the grass to let off a little steam.

Our parents had promised we'd see the ocean and build sand castles on the beach. But all we'd done up to that point was sit for hours strapped in car seats, watching traffic and trees pass by outside the car windows. It seemed like we'd never get to where we were going.

To break up the monotony, Dad suggested, "Let's switch cars."

He set me and my car seat between him and Uncle Doug in the front seat of our big, old, green Chevy Impala. Mom, Jami, and Aunt Kathy all piled into the Rupp's Mercury to follow us. Guys in one car, gals in the other. Pulling back out onto Interstate 95, heading north toward Maine.

We had barely regained interstate speed before the traffic began to slow for the approach to the Hampton Toll Plaza. Dad had taken his wallet out of his pocket, so he and Uncle Doug conducted a frantic search of the front seat to come up with enough cash.

Aunt Kathy eased up behind us even as Dad rolled down his window. With a five-dollar bill in his left hand, he extended his arm to pay the toll. That was the last thing he remembered for several minutes.

At that moment, Uncle Doug heard a loud noise behind us. By the time he turned and looked back to determine what it was, all he could see out the rear window was the front grill of the semi about to hit us.

What none of us knew until later was that an 18-wheel tractor-trailer rig loaded with 80,000 pounds of onions was slamming into our lane of cars. Mom instinctively turned and looked back toward the sound, just in time to see the huge truck plowing into and through the cars lined up behind us. The other vehicles hardly slowed it down before the forty-ton impact shattered the windows and propelled the Rupp's Mercury into and over the rear of our Chevy, where it came to rest crossways on top of the concrete barrier protecting the tollbooth.

For a few seconds Mom tried to clear her head. The truck's initial blow had rammed the Mercury forward with such force that she felt as though her skull had bounced off a cement-block wall instead of the back of her upholstered car seat. But when Mom saw the flames licking up over the back bumper and trunk, all grogginess disappeared. Instinctively, she screamed, "Jami!" When she realized her daughter was crying but unhurt in the backseat, she grabbed Jami and began shouting at my still-dazed aunt, "Kathy! Get out! Get out as fast as you can!"

The impact had twisted the frame of the car so that neither front door would open at first. Mom's side was wedged up against the tollbooth anyway, so they all needed to escape on Kathy's side. They were about to resort to crawling out the window when Kathy finally forced her door open just enough so they could slip out, one at a time, even as Mom screamed, "It's going to blow! It's going to blow!" Then, with Jami's arms clinging to Mom's neck and her legs wrapped around Mom's waist, they sprinted away from the burning wreckage—around and in front of the toll lanes and onto the grass along the road at the edge of the toll plaza.

Meantime, the combined force of the ricocheting Mercury and the 18-wheeler crumpling our Chevy delivered such a violent jolt that my infant seat flipped up and over into the rear of our car where I ended up wedged out of sight behind the back of the front seat even as we spun around 180 degrees. At the same time the gas tank exploded, and the entire automobile burst into flames.

Dad and Uncle Doug were both knocked out. Within moments Dad roused just enough to see I was gone; a wall of flame had already filled his open window. Still only semiconscious, he somehow forced open the door, climbed out through the fire, and staggered away from the wreck. Within seconds, Uncle Doug regained enough of his senses to realize that the car was on fire and he needed to get out. Instinctively he forced open his door. But he could only get it open a few inches, because the passenger side of the car was now jammed against the tollbooth. Unfortunately, the door opened just enough for the flames to shoot through the crack from under the car and to burn his arm and side and face on the right side of his body before he managed to shut the door again. No escape that way!

Looking across the empty front seat he saw more flames. But the driver's-side door appeared to be open. Beyond the flames was an inviting patch of grass. So Doug scrambled across the seat, slid under the steering wheel, dove through the fire, and then rolled on the ground, trying to smother the flames.

By the time Mom got Jami safely away from the burning vehicles and into the grass on the side of the road, it still hadn't registered on her how many cars had been involved. Until my Aunt Kathy first exclaimed, "Where are the guys?" Then, "LOOK!" She pointed toward our green Chevy, which was by then completely engulfed in flames.

Mom and Aunt Kathy could only hold each other and moan, "They're gone!" as they imagined our three bodies trapped inside the fiery wreckage. Then a large man staggered toward them—his face black with soot and smoke, his clothes torn, charred material dangling from his outstretched arms. Mom assumed he was the truck driver and began backing away before Aunt Kathy exclaimed, "Jan! It's Mike!"

"Mike!" Mom shouted in momentary relief. Then, "Where's Joel!"

Dad groaned in response. "He was such a neat son . . ."

At that point Mom began screaming in disbelief and horror, "My baby! My baby!"

While all this was happening—accident victims fleeing the wreckage in shock, even as other people milled around gawking—a few folks had the presence of mind to take action. One of the tollbooth attendants grabbed a fire extinguisher and began spraying it on the flames.

He heard Mom's screams and called to her, "Which car is your baby in?" She pointed to the Chevy, and he turned his extinguisher on our green Impala.

"If someone will get the baby, I'll cover you," the attendant said, continuing to discharge a stream of foamy chemicals over the blaze.

I don't know what he heard first—Mom's screams, my crying, or the urgent instructions of the tollbooth attendant. But one young bystander by the name of Michael Saraceni, realizing that I was still inside, ran right up to the scorching heat, reached past the flames, grabbed my fast-melting car seat with his bare hands, and snatched me from the fire. With his own hands badly blistered, he carried me over to where my mother stood crying before he let go and dropped the molten car seat to the ground.

Aunt Kathy had watched the man reach into the car to get me. She said that when he ran up with the car seat I looked like a burned marshmallow.

Even through her grief-stricken sobs, Mom says she noticed the thud of the car seat on the grassy ground. Then she heard the warning tone of Kathy's voice saying, "Jan? It's Joel." There, on the ground, sat a smoldering infant seat holding a small body charred beyond recognition.

Mom handed Jami to Kathy and knelt down for a closer look. "Joel?"

My face was black. All my hair gone. The top of my head white. My eyelids were burned shut and had begun to swell. My nose looked black and shriveled. What was left looked both puffy and shrunken, hardly even recognizable as a face.

"Joel?" Mom asked, not wanting to believe it was me. But there was no real doubt. She recognized the half-burned baby shoes she'd dressed me in for the trip that morning. Mom reached out to take my arm but quickly let go. My skin was still so hot she couldn't bear to even touch me.

"Oh, Joel, Joel, Joel!" she sobbed.

As a nurse Mom had been around a lot of suffering. She certainly didn't want me to experience that. She knew death would bring an end to the pain. Even as she thought about that, she pictured me walking and holding hands with God in heaven and thought, *Joel would be a lot better off if he died.*

This was about the time Michael Saraceni grabbed her arm to tell her, "I saved your baby, lady. I saved your baby. He's going to be all right."

Mom says that, as she looked at me and saw the extent of my burns, she wanted to scream at this stranger for his role in prolonging my pain. *You don't know what you're talking about! He's going to die! Why did you save him?*

But all she said was a quiet thank-you between her sobs, as she quickly shifted into nursing mode and tried to decide what to do for her son. She wasn't sure I was even breathing at first. So she blew a quick breath of air into my blackened mouth. I choked and coughed and began to scream.

Almost twenty years later a paramedic who worked the scene said he had never been able to forget the sound of those screams. And he hoped he would never hear screams like that from a human being again.

One of the ambulance attendants poured a pitcher of cold water over my burned torso. So much steam rose when the water contacted my body that it scared my mother. But a doctor who'd run up from where the traffic was backing up on I-95 said to keep pouring water over me to cool my body and stop the progressive damage caused by the heat.

As I continued screaming in terror and pain, the only comfort Mom could give me was to let me know I wasn't alone. "Mommy's here!" she sobbed. "Mommy's here, Joel."

From where he sat slumped against the wall of the building containing the tollbooth offices, Uncle Doug says he remembers hearing and recognizing my dad's voice crying out, "My son! My son!"

Everyone was so focused on me that it took a while for them to notice anyone else. Again it was Aunt Kathy who announced, "Jan! Mike's hurt!"

Dad had his arms around Mom, trying to comfort her. But one of those arms was badly burned, and blood was streaming out of a gash on the back of his head, running down his neck, and dripping into Mom's hair. Uncle Doug was hurt as well. He was dazed and disoriented and had suffered second-degree burns to his face and arms. But his burns didn't look as bad as Dad's did.

Dad was in such pain that Aunt Kathy grabbed an empty trash can and filled it with water for Dad to stick his arms in. After she did the same for Doug, Dad asked her to find a phone to call Nyack College, where he taught biology, and to ask everyone there to pray. Using a phone in the toll plaza office, she got the number from directory assistance and within moments ended up talking to the college switchboard operator. "I don't even know who to ask for," she told the lady. Then she quickly explained what had happened and asked the operator to inform all the appropriate people.

While Kathy was still inside, more emergency vehicles raced up from every direction. Sirens screamed. But none of them any louder than I did. "Let's lift him into the back of the ambulance," a paramedic instructed my mother. Using my charred infant seat as a stretcher, he and my mother ran for the nearest ambulance.

Mom wanted to help care for me. But the EMTs made her sit in the front of the cab as they raced to the local hospital. In the back I continued to scream. And as the flustered, frustrated attendant struggled to get the oxygen hooked up and running, the doctor who was with us tried to reassure him. "Don't worry. This kid's not going to make it anyway."

No one who saw me could have disagreed.

Chapter 3

The medical staff in the ER at Exeter Hospital certainly didn't have much hope. While the doctors frantically thumbed through medical books to determine what immediate medical intervention they could provide for such a critically burned child, my mother stopped at a pay phone and made two quick calls. First to her mother in Michigan and then to Dad's mother in Florida. Mom told them where we were and what had happened, and she asked them to please begin praying.

While the doctors there never expected me to live, they knew if I had any chance of surviving, I would need to be transferred immediately to a larger hospital with a burn unit. Even before Mom got inside the examination room, one of them hurried out to tell her, "We're transferring your son to Boston as soon as possible."

The rest of our family were on their way to the Exeter Hospital emergency room. My aunt and Jami found Mom first. Mom hugged and tried to comfort my sister, even as she filled Kathy in on the plans to immediately move me to Boston. As she talked, her predicament sank in.

How could she leave with me for Boston? She had no money. (Her purse had burned up in the car.) She didn't even have any clothes to change into. (All the suitcases were also gone.) Uncle Doug and Dad were being rushed to Exeter for treatment of their injuries. Aunt Kathy had no money or clothes either; she had no place to stay. And what about Jami?

19

While Mom and Aunt Kathy tried to figure out what to do, a blonde woman in her thirties walked up and introduced herself. "My name is Nancy MacKenzie," she said. "I'm a lab technician here at the hospital. I couldn't help overhearing. I want to help."

Nancy told my aunt, "You can come and stay at my house." Then she turned to my mother. "Your little girl is welcome too. My teenage daughter and I will help take good care of her."

Mom accepted the gracious offer and quickly knelt down by Jami to give her a reassuring hug and try to explain what was happening. That Jami was going to stay with Aunt Kathy for a while because Joel was badly hurt and needed Mommy to go with him. That they would visit some new friends. That Daddy was going to stay at this hospital, and Jami would get to talk to him on the phone and maybe even visit him while he was there. Then Mom said a quick good-bye to my sister and rushed off to find Dad.

The doctors were still trying to assess Dad's burns when Mom walked into the exam room to tell him, "They are transferring Joel to Boston!"

"You have to go with him," he told her.

Mom knew that, but she didn't want to leave Dad and Jami.

"How is Jami?"

"She's fine." Mom told him about Kathy and Nancy MacKenzie offering to take care of her.

"Go with Joel," Dad insisted.

"They don't think he's going to live," Mom told him as she began to cry.

"I know," Dad replied. "We were so lucky to have him for two years. He had the neatest personality—so much fun." They were both crying as they held each other.

"We need to pray," Dad said. And then he began. "Thank you, Lord, for Joel. Thank you for giving him to us. He was so neat. He was a gift. Thank you for every day that you gave him into our care. We ask, Lord, that your will be done with his life. And thank you for saving the rest of us from this accident. Amen." Years later, one of the nurses who was in the room said that, by the time Dad had finished praying, even the medical staff had tears running down their faces. (The head nurse in the Exeter ER would resign after that night and go to work in a doctor's office because she never again wanted to witness a case like mine.)

Within minutes an aide found my mother to tell her, "The ambulance is leaving for Boston, Mrs. Sonnenberg." Mom rushed out to the ER waiting room only to discover that the ambulance had already pulled out.

I screamed at the top of my lungs until my ambulance was halfway to Boston; then I suddenly stopped. The nurse riding with me thought maybe I had died. Or was about to. Not knowing what else to do, she grabbed a bottle of intravenous solution and poured it over my torso. The shock started me screaming again, and I kept up the racket for the rest of the hour-long ride into the city.

Back in Exeter, a firefighter walked into the ER waiting room and generously handed Mom a handful of coins to make phone calls. When she explained that she didn't know how she was going to get to Boston, he told her he and his wife would drive her. So Nancy MacKenzie handed her a $20 bill, and a little over an hour later Mom finally caught up with me at Boston Children's Hospital.

I was already in surgery by the time she arrived. Soon a doctor came out to tell her, "We just performed an escharotomy on your son."

"A what?" In all of her nurse's training she couldn't remember having heard of such a thing.

He explained that the burned tissue on the outside of my body acted like a hardened cast. As my extremities began to swell, that stiff shell worked like a tourniquet, cutting off the circulation to any living, unburned tissue underneath. So they actually slit my arms and legs, cutting through and spreading the hard, charred, dead outer tissue to relieve the pressure underneath. "Since you're a nurse," he said, "I don't have to tell you how serious your son's injuries are." He sighed heavily and shook his head sadly. "This is complete devastation—complete devastation." As Mom began to cry, tears welled up in his eyes as well.

"What are Joel's chances?" Mom wanted to know.

"Well, he has third-degree burns over 85 percent of his body. I'd say he has a 10 percent chance at most."

Ten percent! That was more than Mom had hoped for. She told the doctor, "I know you've heard this before, but I want you to know you're working on a very strong child. If there is any chance to survive this, I'm sure Joel can do it. . . . Do you believe in miracles?"

"Well, I've seen the unexplainable," the doctor told her. "So I guess you could say I believe in miracles."

Mom looked up at him and said, "I want you to know I believe in them. And I believe a miracle can happen. I don't know if it will, but God can do a miracle for my son. I want you to know ahead of time, so that when it happens, you'll know we were looking for it."

If any miracle was going to take place, everyone understood the first twenty-four hours would be key. All of the bodily fluids that had shifted into my surviving tissue had to be quickly replenished intravenously. If I survived that, there would be a new danger of overloading my circulatory system while my body spent the next several days reabsorbing into the bloodstream the fluid from the swollen tissue.

"I believe a miracle can happen. I don't know if it will, but God can do a miracle for my son."

The doctor assured Mom they would monitor my fluids and my kidney function very carefully. He explained that if I survived those first two crises, the most serious concern of all would be infection. "That will be his biggest battle after the first few days, and it will last for weeks and weeks," the doctor said. "Your son is going to have a long fight—if he makes it through these next few days."

I surprised my doctors by surviving Saturday night. And Sunday morning tens of thousands of people in churches across the country prayed for me and my family. Back in Nyack, at our own church, the pastor led the congregation in prayer, saying, "Lord, we don't have any answers, just questions of 'why?' But amidst all these whys, we remember that you are God. You have created us. You are in control of us. We lift up to you this morning the Sonnenberg family in their great need. And little Joel—we can't imagine what he is going through. We know that you do know, though, and that he is in your almighty hands. We pray for Mike, Jan, and Jami today, for their comfort and strength, Lord. Joel's injury is so severe that we really don't know how to pray with any wisdom. We don't know which would be better—if he were to live, or if he should go home to be with you. We ask only that your will be done in this precious child's life. Amen."

For the time being the doctors could do little for me but wait and watch how I responded. Amazingly, my vital signs stabilized, though my condition continued to be listed as critical. My family's situation, however, seemed far from stable.

Dad remained in the Exeter Hospital, where his head had swollen to the size of a basketball and his severely burned hand was also several times larger than normal. He fielded a constant string of phone calls, talking to Mom about my condition, responding to messages from family and friends, and dictating instructions about insurance and other business details related to everything from his teaching schedule at Nyack College to the accident itself.

The MacKenzies were entertaining Jami, as Nancy had promised they would do. Uncle Doug remained hospitalized for his burns. Aunt Kathy continued to help care for both her brother and her husband. Both of my grandmothers flew to Boston—Grandma Sonnenberg from Florida to be with Dad in Exeter, and Grandma Schneider from Michigan to be with Mom and me in Boston.

So many people wanted to help. A Nyack professor and her husband left their own baby with grandparents and drove up to Boston to see what they could do. Sunday morning they went looking for stores where they could buy clothes, shoes, makeup, toiletries, a purse, pens, paper, and anything else they thought my mother would need. Another one of Mom's good friends, a woman who also was a critical care nurse, came to be with us and to help look out for my care. Sunday afternoon a young couple from our home church drove to Boston to bring money, cards, messages, clothes, and more gifts for the entire family.

At my mother's request they had brought a big 8 x 10 inch portrait of Jami and me, which Mom promptly hung over the head of my bed so that every medical person who came into the room could look beyond my charred corpse and see the cute, smiling little boy for whom they were caring.

I survived a second night.

My eyelids had been burned so severely and my entire face was so swollen that there was serious concern my eyes might have been damaged beyond repair. That's why an ophthalmologist showed up early Monday morning to examine me. Mom feared the worst. Instead the doctor sighed and said, "Well, it looks like just minor burns to the corneas, the one eye more extensive than the other."

Mom got so excited she couldn't wait to call Dad and tell him the good news. September 17 was his birthday, and she couldn't think of a better surprise gift than telling him his son would be able to see.

A short time later, when a plastic surgeon made his rounds, Mom came right out and asked him, "What can be done for Joel from your point of view?"

He told her the most important thing was to get me transferred across town to the Shriners Burn Institute, where they did pioneering work in saving children with serious burns like mine. "Time is of the essence," he said. "Joel's injuries have to be covered with skin. This needs to be done as fast and as expertly as possible if you want to save your son's life.

"What they will do is shave off and use the skin that hasn't been burned for the grafts. Your son has small areas of unburned skin remaining on his lower back, abdomen, and buttocks. Those will need to be the donor sites, areas that will provide good skin to cover the rest of Joel's body. These autografts will need to be sutured in place, where they will eventually grow onto and over the wounded tissue, healing in about ten days.

"In massive burns, such as Joel's, where a large area must be covered with skin taken from a much smaller area, numerous grafts will have to be taken from the same spot. This is called cropping. The healthy skin is sliced off, or harvested, in very thin layers again and again—as quickly as it grows back."

Because there was so little undamaged skin left on my body to use, the plastic surgeon explained that the skin would be stretched to its maximum surface area by a process called meshing, in which tiny holes would be poked in it—like a mesh screen or nylon stockings. He reemphasized that what mattered most was speed. The sooner the dead, germ-infested, burned tissue was removed from my body and my injuries covered with new skin, the better would be my chances of fighting off deadly infection.

The doctor told Mom, "The treatment must begin soon. There is a ten- to fourteen-day lag during which the donor sites must heal before being cropped again. And a lot of germs can grow in two weeks. So at the Shriners Burn Institute they've pioneered the use of a skin bank; in fact, they had the first operational skin bank in the country. They take skin from other people to provide temporary coverage for the burn patient. They could even take skin from you or your husband, which would stay on longer than skin taken from other people. This is the only place in the world I know of where they're using parental skin effectively to provide temporary coverage. Any grafts taken from other individuals will eventually be rejected by Joel's body, but they will buy time for him by reducing the percentage of body surface still open to the air until the doctors can harvest enough of his own skin. And that will reduce the risk of infection." He didn't have to remind Mom that infection was the greatest danger I would face.

She wanted to know: "What are Joel's chances of living if he's transferred to the Burn Institute?"

"As soon as he is covered with skin—a combination of his own and from the skin bank—maybe 70 percent."

Finally a real sense of hope. "When can he go?"

"There may be a bed opening up tomorrow or Wednesday."

Grandma Schneider insisted she would stay in Boston with me on Monday so Mom could go back to Exeter to visit Dad on his birthday, tell him what she'd learned from the doctors, and share a little time with Jami. So the rest of the family held a party in my father's hospital room—singing "Happy Birthday," opening gifts, and eating a cake Nancy MacKenzie and Jami had baked and decorated.

Someone had clipped out the local newspaper article from *Foster's Daily Democrat:*

HAMPTON CRASH YIELDS CHARGE

Hampton—A trucker from Nova Scotia was scheduled to be arraigned in Hampton District Court this morning on a charge of aggravated assault in connection with a fiery chain-reaction accident at the Hampton toll-booth Saturday afternoon that sent nine people to area hospitals.

Reginald H. Dort, of Nova Scotia, was arrested and held in lieu of $25,000 cash bail after his tractor-trailer truck slammed into a row of passenger cars waiting to pay tolls at the I-95 interchange. Dort said the brakes on the truck failed just before it struck the rear of an auto driven by Bonnie Lynn Dunn of North Andover, Massachusetts.

State Police Sgt. Sheldon P. Sullivan said Dort was held pending a determination if the brakes indeed failed. State police impounded the vehicles in the crash and were to inspect the autos today.

Four persons remain hospitalized this morning. Most seriously injured . . . Joel Sonnenberg of South Nyack, N.Y., who was listed in poor condition at Boston Children's Hospital with burns over 75 percent of his body.

Two of the autos involved in the accident caught fire on impact.

"It looked like a battle scene," said a motorist who arrived after the accident. "Two cars were charred, another was sliced in half. . . ."

Three of the victims remained in Exeter Hospital this morning. Michael Sonnenberg, 33, father of Joel Sonnenberg, and Douglas L.

Rupp, 27, of Archbold, Ohio were listed in good condition. Mrs. Dunn,
21, was listed in stable condition.

Five other persons were treated and released at the hospital
Saturday for injuries received in the accident.

The accident tangled northbound traffic on the heavily used interstate for hours, police said.*

Everyone read the article and wondered what it meant, because it raised more
questions than it answered. What was the "aggravated assault" charge all about?
It didn't become public until later that the truck driver may have spent the previous night with the woman in the first car he hit. Or that investigators speculated she may have been on her way to Canada to tell Dort's wife when he tried
to stop her by ramming her car.

After the birthday celebration, my parents discussed what the plastic surgeon had
said and agreed to transfer me to Shriners. The doctors also determined that my
father should be the one to donate skin to be grafted over my wounds. So Dad
began making plans to transfer to Boston so he could be near me and Mom.

In the meantime, he found a creative way to make his presence felt in my
hospital room. He gave Mom a cassette tape with a message he'd recorded for me.

The first thing she did when she got back to Boston was to tell me all about
the party. How much everyone had missed me and that Dad and Jami sent their
love. Because I was wrapped tight like a mummy, my arms and legs splinted out
straight and a ventilator tube down my throat breathing for me, she had no idea
whether or not I could hear and understand what she was saying.

But then she said, "I have a very special present for you, Joel—from Daddy.
He wants to talk to you. Do you want to talk with Daddy?"

I nodded my head, ever so slightly. Mom wondered if she was just seeing
things. Maybe it was wishful thinking. When she told the nurses I'd nodded my
head, they looked at her like she was crazy. But just in case, she quickly started
the tape.

*"Hampton Crash Yields Charge," *Foster's Daily Democrat*, Dover, N.H., September 16, 1979.
Reprinted with permission.

Dad's voice filled the hospital room:

▶▶▎ Joel, how are you, son? I love you so much. You know I've been missing you. Wish we could see each other. It'd be a lot of fun being near you. Remember how we would go out in the backyard and get our hammers out and hammer on the blocks of wood? That's a lot of fun, isn't it?

▶▶▎ Remember, too, how we'd go down to the woodpile, and you'd help me split the logs and carry the logs to the big woodpile? We have to get you out of the hospital quick so you can come home and do all that stuff.

▶▶▎ Remember one of your favorite things to do was to go in the sandbox and make big sand castles? You know how big that sandbox is with all the sand in it. Boy, you'd take your trucks and move them around and up and down. Sometimes you'd even take your tricycle and drive it all the way from the house to the big sandbox. That was something else!

▶▶▎ You know, when we get out of this hospital, we're going to go for more hikes. Remember how you used to get way up on my shoulders, and I'd lift you high up in the sky? In fact, you had to watch out 'cause when we walked through doorways we always had to duck down or you'd bump your head. Then we'd go walking outside, and we'd hike and hike and hike. Remember how you used to rub my head and my hair so softly and gently, making Daddy feel so good? Yeah, that was lots of fun, wasn't it?

▶▶▎ Remember how under the beech tree there was a hole in the ground? We'd put our ears down to the ground and listen to hear the trickle of water. Do you remember how much we liked to listen to the water? That was such a neat sound! We'll have times like that again, you know.

▶▶▎ Then Daddy would go into the biology lab. Sometimes when he wasn't thinking too much, he'd even take you into the biology lab. You'd come into the room and get in one drawer and then another and another. Remember your favorite thing to do? You'd take those rubber stoppers and throw them around the room.

▶▶▎ Funny boy! You liked to be outside so much. It's pretty tough being inside, isn't it? I know it's tough, but we'll get out of here and do a lot more hiking soon.

▶▶▎ You know another thing we need to talk about, Joel? Remember your big truck book that you liked so much? It had big pictures of trucks with headlights and wheels. Remember how you liked all those funny people driving those trucks? Remember how you would take Daddy by the hand, have him sit down on the mattress, put a book in his hand, jump up on the bed right beside him, and then with our backs against the wall we would go through the whole book? Wasn't that lots of fun?

▶▶❙ Daddy seems to be all talked out for a little while. Boy, am I ever excited to talk to you again. Pretty soon I'll be talking to you again, and we can tell secrets to each other—things that nobody else will know. Okay? I love you very much. Lots of hugs and kisses. Rest easy now.

The next day my mother decided to make a tape of her own. But since she was around and could talk to me herself, she decided to record herself singing some of the songs she used to sing to calm me down and get me to sleep. One of those songs that seemed especially appropriate to the circumstances contained the following lyrics:

> I am a promise. I am a possibility!
> I am a promise, with a capital "P."
> I'm a great big bundle of potentiality.
> And I am learnin' to hear God's voice
> And I am tryin' to make the right choice.
> I am a promise to be . . . anything God wants me to be.
>
> I can go anywhere He wants me to go,
> I can be anything that He wants me to be.
> I can climb the high mountain, I can cross the wide sea.
> I'm a great big promise you see!*

When I heard my parents' recordings, I started moving my legs. First up and down slowly. Then more vigorously. Slamming them up and down on the bed. Obviously trying to communicate in the only way I could, until finally the doctors had to sedate me.

I don't know what I was trying to say. Neither do I remember what I was feeling as I listened to those tapes. But I can tell you this: among the most vivid and

*I Am a Promise. Words by William J. and Gloria Gaither. Music by William J. Gaither. Copyright © 1975 William J. Gaither, Inc. All rights controlled by Gaither Copyright Management. Used by permission.

lasting memories of my childhood are the sounds of my parents' voices. Even when I couldn't see them or respond to them, they were always there. With me. Encouraging me and assuring me that everything was going to be okay.

But would everything be okay? The medical outcome was still far from certain. The strain on my family those first few days was terrible. And it didn't get any better as they began to realize that the ordeal had only just begun.

Money had been the least of anyone's concerns to start with. But on Wednesday morning, in a meeting with a hospital social worker, Mom asked: "How do families cope with the constant drain on their financial resources over a long period of time?"

"You shouldn't have too much problem with that once Joel is transferred," the caseworker replied. "The Shriners Burn Institute is free." She explained that it was funded by the work of local Shriners organizations from all over the country.

That was wonderful news. Better yet was the word that a bed had opened up at Shriners and I would be transferred the very next day.

Mom explained what was happening. That I was being moved to a new hospital. A better place, with other children who were also sick. That a doctor and some nurses were going with me. The new hospital wasn't far away. The trip would take just a few minutes. "And Mommy will be there too."

Of course, I don't remember being transferred. Or my first impressions of the new hospital, which was to become a very familiar place throughout my childhood. But the staff of Boston's Shriners Burn Institute certainly remember my arrival.

Betty Dew, who was to become my primary care nurse, has never forgotten our first encounter. "I had just started working at Shriners after working with burn patients in Orlando for several years. When I walked into the admission room, I saw this toddler lying there, and I walked over to you. What I remember most were the hands—little baby hands and fingers. And when I reached down to touch those fingers, they were as hard as stone. They looked and felt like the hands of a rigid plastic doll. I almost passed out."

More than twenty years later, this veteran nurse choked up as she told how she'd cared for lots of burn patients—but nothing she'd ever seen prepared her for me. "You probably had the most severe injuries of any surviving burn patient in the world up to that time. The burns all over your body weren't the worst— it was the burns through your skull. Our doctors began calling all over the world—Europe, China—trying to find someone, anyone, who had ever treated a burn patient with that kind of injury to the skull.

"No one with such severe burns had ever lived."

C h a p t e r 4

At Shriners I was immediately placed in a plastic tent called a Bacteria-Controlled Nursing Unit (BCNU), which had been developed by that hospital. In my ward there were four of these big, bulky units, each containing one severely burned child.

The smooth, thick plastic sides of my tent ran from ceiling to floor around my bed, completely isolating me. Air was pumped in at the top of the unit, filtered to make it bacteria-free before it flowed over me, and then filtered again as it passed out of the system near the floor. Temperature and humidity were also carefully controlled.

The point, of course, was to reduce the danger of infection by isolating me from the germs of other patients, visitors, and staff until enough protective skin could be grown and harvested to completely cover my burns. This sterile treatment was one of the big reasons for the success Shriners had with burn patients. The protection from germs had proved to be a successful strategy.

What wasn't so good about the BCNUs was that, in isolating me from germs, they also isolated me from people. Every visitor (including my mother) and every staff person who came into the room had to don a plastic gown; pull on long plastic sleeves, a pair of bulky gloves, then a pair of tight surgical gloves over that; and finally put on a mask—before they could even approach my bed. To touch me, move me, change my diaper, or treat my wounds, they had to reach through slits in the plastic that would muffle voices and distort any view I had of the people moving around outside my bubble.

I wasn't yet moving around much inside the tent. A respirator tube ran down my throat. My arms and legs were splinted outward and wrapped with heavy bandages so that I was spread-eagle on the bed. My head was wrapped, as were my chest and back. The only place I wasn't bandaged was the unburned area of my body that had been covered by a wet diaper during the accident.

It was from small unburned areas on my tummy, lower back, and buttocks that doctors would have to harvest enough skin to completely cover the rest of my body. And because time was critical, they scheduled my first operation, my first grafting, the day after I arrived at Shriners. Step one was to cover my back, which had been almost totally burned, with skin taken from a small area on my abdomen. First, the eschar (charred tissue) had to be scraped or cut away. Then they sliced a thin layer of skin off my stomach, meshed and stretched it as far as possible, and stitched it over the exposed tissues of my back.

Since they grafted such a large area, I lost more than four pints of blood—almost twice the total volume of blood a toddler like me even had. But it was important for my body to "take" as much skin with each graft as possible. The longer it took for me to get a complete covering of new skin, the greater the risk of deadly infection.

Three days later I underwent another operation—this one to cover my chest. Much of the damage to my back had been done where my plastic car seat had melted and fused into my flesh. The ER doctors had struggled to literally pry and pull me out of the cooling car seat after I arrived at the hospital in Exeter. So the burns on my back were bad enough.

But the burns on my chest, which had been exposed directly to the flames, were deeper and even more extensive. So in this second operation I again lost a large amount of blood.

Four days later, doctors covered my legs, which were burned all the way around, with skin grafts taken from my dad's thighs. The doctors explained to my parents that this temporary graft would not only protect me from germs; it would also help prepare the underlying tissue to receive a later graft of my own skin. Operation after operation followed as they covered each of my arms with more temporary grafts of my father's skin.

To keep me from rejecting the donated skin right away, the doctors administered a drug that lowered my body's ability to fight off foreign objects. That immunosuppressant greatly improved the odds of Dad's skin lasting until enough of my own skin could be harvested and grafted over my wounds. But at the same time the drug reduced my body's ability to fight off germs and therefore increased the danger of infection.

For weeks the doctors constantly tinkered with my body's immune system, trying to find the balance that would preserve the skin and prevent serious infections. While the nurses tried to maintain my temperature at a fairly constant 101 degrees, because they'd found that to be the optimum condition for healing, my temp peaked at 104 to 105 most afternoons and soared again during the night. Whenever my body overheated, I'd get so restless that the nurses would tie my hands and my feet to the sides of the bed to keep me from thrashing around and hurting myself further.

During one operation surgeons cropped almost three square feet of unburned skin from Dad's thighs to use as grafts to cover his own burns as well as mine. While I don't remember the pain from the donor sites, my father does. And it was excruciatingly painful—like holding a hot iron against the skin for days with no relief.

Betty Dew said, "You were definitely a fighter. And I saw that as an encouraging sign—your best hope."

Not only did I thrash around violently when I ran a temp or was hurting especially bad, but I would very deliberately act out my anger toward my mother. I was too young to understand the rules for visiting hours, so I'd get upset when she had to leave. And when she came back, I experienced conflicting emotions.

"Every day for some time you'd lie very still in bed, just waiting for your mother to arrive," Betty remembered. "When she walked in and greeted you, you would turn your head just enough to make eye contact. And you'd wait. Not reacting. Not even moving. Just staring at your mom. She'd be talking sweetly to you, and you still wouldn't move. She'd get closer, and you'd just lie there, waiting—your arms splinted out from your sides. Your mom would reach into the tent with her plastic gloves. Still you didn't move—until she leaned in far enough to reach out and touch you. Then, like lightning, you somehow twisted your whole bandaged body toward her so that the splinted arm on the far side of your body rotated up and over to WHACK your mother on the head.

"It was hard for her not to take that as a sign of personal rejection. But I kept telling her it was the only way you could express your frustration and unhappiness about her being gone. And it was the only way at that time for you to express your anger over the terrible pain you were in. Everything we had to do to help you caused even more terrible pain, and you were just too young to understand."

I did understand that my days consisted of constant agony and frustration over feeling helplessly confined. I don't know which was worse. I hated both. And I did everything within my power, as limited as it was, to express my feelings.

Early in October I gained a new means of expressing myself when the respirator tube came out of my throat. I'd used a few words to communicate before the accident. But as is often the case with children who experience trauma, I had almost completely regressed. In a scratchy, raspy voice I cried for "Daddy! Daddy! Daddy!"—the one person unable to be at my bedside. That one word was now my total vocabulary.

However, after weeks without use of my vocal cords, I could now cry out loud and scream. So I did scream. It was my chance to be heard.

"To begin with, most of the staff believed your burned skull was a death sentence," Betty said. "But when we pulled out the respirator tube and I heard you scream, I never again doubted you were gonna make it. I always worried about those kids who didn't cry. But you were a screamer.

"No one in the hospital made as much noise as you did. I don't remember a quiet day with you. And that encouraged me. On the other hand, there were days when that constant screaming discouraged me. I hated to see you suffer like that. But I sure liked your spunk!"

I discovered a new sense of freedom with the respirator tube out. And I wanted more. Though still bound hand and foot in heavy, stiff splints, I would stand up in my bed, screaming and thrashing and pulling the feeding tube out of my nose. I wanted out of bed, out of that tent. Out!

And I couldn't understand why no one would let me out. I had had enough confinement, enough hospitals, enough nurses, and enough pain. Thankfully, I didn't understand how far I had yet to go.

Betty Dew said one reason she believed I would survive was because I was too young to understand. "An adult would have died for sure with your injuries," she said, "because an adult would know the seriousness and the long-range implications. They would not only have the pain but also the realization of what was to come. But you were just a baby. You didn't worry about the future. You could just concentrate on fighting and surviving another day."

Some of those days seemed pretty discouraging to those people caring for me—when I began losing body parts, for example.

"I knew you wouldn't keep your fingers and toes," Betty Dew told me. "There just wasn't any living tissue left there. The fourth-degree burns had gone all the way through the bone.

"Even so, it took time for the damaged and dead tissue to come off. It was probably one day in mid-October when I was changing your sheets and found the first finger. The next day I found another. Then a toe. At first we saved them in a petri dish and sent them to our lab. Then we just started throwing them out with the trash.

"Cleaning your face one day your lip came off. The ears probably came off before that. And then your nose. There was nothing we could do. The damage had been too great from the beginning."

As upsetting as it was for my mom to see me literally going to pieces in front of her eyes—as worried as my parents were about how I would cope without fingers, without toes, without normal facial features—all that useless, charred, germ-infested, dead tissue had to come off before the rest of my body could heal. My survival depended on it.

The grafting operations continued. Four days after I came off the respirator, my feet were covered with my own skin. The next day my dad was allowed to leave his hospital and visit me for the first time since the accident. Four days later Dad was released from the hospital for good because it looked like I wouldn't need any more of his skin.

On October 22 my right leg was covered with my own skin. Three days later the doctors grafted my own skin over my left leg. And four days after that, my upper right arm was covered with my own skin.

Despite the success of the grafts so far, Betty Dew told me that two real problem areas remained: "Your left arm had been burned so badly that not only the fingers came off but your hand disintegrated as well, piece by piece, until just a stub of forearm remained. Right at the end of the stump, where your wrist would have been, we could see an exposed artery pulsing. It had been soldered shut by the burn. But there it was, right at the surface at the end of your arm. We kept a blood pressure cuff on that arm for a long time so that if it burst we could immediately tighten the cuff like a tourniquet to keep you from bleeding to death. It would have been a major bleed, and you were so small you didn't have that much blood to lose. We kept the end of your arm wrapped and heavily padded because it took a long time for it to heal enough to cover with a skin graft. And until then we worried, because that artery looked so scary.

"The biggest concern of all, however, was the burn on top of your head. When dead bone tissue began sloughing off your exposed skull, we worried that the entire thickness of skull would come off in places. But it never did. So much of the skull was burned that, when it did break off, there were spots where there was so little bone left that I could see what looked like brain tissue underneath. We worried that any infection there might be deadly. But we didn't know what to do other than keep the wound clean.

"How do you grow bone? In surgery they drilled little holes into the healthy portions of your skull to try to stimulate growth. And that seemed to do something, because it wasn't long before the top of your head had little bumps that reminded me of seedlings growing."

Still the skull remained exposed.

Thanksgiving fell on my birthday that year. I turned two on November 22, 1979. Our hometown paper wrote about our celebration in a feature article titled "Family's Thanks Stem from Son's Survival":

> Many American families today will gather together to ask the Lord's blessing. One from South Nyack will not.
>
> Mike and Janet Sonnenberg and their children, Jami and Joel, will spend the day in a Boston children's hospital. They will enjoy a sumptuous turkey dinner, although Joel will eat his while peering out at his parents and sister from the inside of a bacteria-resistant plastic tent.
>
> Joel has no fingers or toes. He has lost his ears, nose, eyelids, and lips. His body is covered with skin grafted from the tiny portions where the skin did not burn off in an automobile accident in Hampton, N.H., in September.
>
> But the Sonnenbergs won't ask the Lord's blessing, because they will be too busy today giving thanks for the rich rewards they feel they already enjoy.

Joel, you see, is still alive. He turns two years old today. Weeks ago, just after the accident, he was not expected to live. No one has ever survived this long before after being burned as badly as little Joel Sonnenberg.

And for Mike, 33, a professor of anatomy, physiology, and biology at Nyack College, it seems that no one has ever been as richly blessed with the love and generosity of others as the Sonnenberg family.

"We'd have to be among the more thankful people this Thanksgiving," Mike said Tuesday, reached by phone at his Boston lodgings, the home of a family he had never met before the accident—one of the many families that have reached out since September to the Sonnenbergs. . . .

While the Shriners doctors worked on Joel, using experimental techniques and technologies that did not exist as recently as two years ago, the Sonnenberg family found itself adrift in New England. Coming from Michigan, they didn't have any friends or relatives in that part of the country. But there were other people who did, and strangers quickly became friends, as what Janet calls the "Christian network" went to work.

"The day of the accident," said Mike, "I was in the hospital, and when my wife and son went to Boston, our daughter, Jami, had no place to go. So a lady took her in and kept her for a week, and when she came back to us, she had no fear or trauma about the whole accident.

"Grace Conservative Baptist Church in Nanuet purchased us a car. Friends through the church helped us financially, got us clothes. The Park Street Church in Boston found Janet a place to stay. And people keep coming up from the churches to visit us—people we don't even know."

"We're having a neat Thanksgiving," Janet said, "because we can really identify with the Pilgrim fathers, who were so grateful for the basic necessities. We're so thankful for Joel's life. . . ."*

The Wednesday after Thanksgiving my face was covered by a graft of my own skin. One day the week after that, my temperature spiked so high it didn't register on the thermometer. "We were still checking your vital signs every hour," recalled Betty Dew. "One hour it was right where we wanted it, then an hour later it was off the charts. We actually had to send to the lab for an animal thermometer to take it. I don't remember how high it went, but it was beyond the

*"Family's Thanks Stem from Son's Survival," *Journal News*, November 22, 1979. Copyright © *The Journal News*. Reprinted with permission.

range of 'living.' We immediately packed you in ice and got the fever down. For a while we feared you'd contracted some sort of brain infection. But we never did figure out what caused the problem."

Three days later I was sitting up in bed, hammering on pegs and laughing. The day after that I took my first walk—inside the tent, back and forth right beside my bed.

As the holidays approached, my parents sent out their annual Christmas letter. But this one was different from the usual "Season's Greetings." They told about the accident and gave a quick accounting of all that had happened with me since, reporting highlights of my recovery—including the more than fifteen surgeries so far. They ended the letter this way:

> *We are awed by Joel's progress in the last three months. We have witnessed a miracle. We are indeed thankful and humbled by all of you dear friends who have helped us out. Your calls, cards, gifts, and most importantly your prayers, have made all the difference. Our prayer requests for future months are as follows:*
>
> *1. For another miracle—that Joel's skull bone may heal and not have to be removed.*
>
> *2. That he can come out of his "plastic house" soon.*
>
> *3. For family unity despite physical separation.*
>
> *We are grateful to God this Christmas season, who through no accident freely gave His Only Son. May He fill your hearts with the joy of His Gift.*
>
> —*The Sonnenbergs*

On December 14, after yet another operation—this one on the back of my head—I was finally moved out of the tent. Two and a half weeks later I was moved to the hospital's rehabilitation ward. Ten days after the move doctors performed an operation on my mouth and eye. They moved and reconstructed my lower lip so that I could eat without having food fall out of my mouth. Then they enclosed my right eye by reconstructing an upper and lower eyelid.

According to my nurse, despite the ongoing procedures, I really enjoyed finally being out of the tent, where I could get face-to-face contact. "You were a hugger," Betty Dew told me, "even more than most kids. When your mom couldn't be there she'd always call and talk to me to get an update. She'd ask me to tell you what everyone in the family was doing. And then she expected me to relay the ritual good-night hugs. I'd walk over to your bed and tell you your family loved you. And I'd ask, 'Do you want a hug from Mommy?' Sometimes if you were upset, you might shake your head. But usually you said, 'Yes,' and I'd give you the hug. Then I'd say, 'Do you want a hug from Daddy?' And I'd give you another big hug. 'Do you want a hug from Jami?' You almost always wanted that one. 'Do you want a hug from your turtle?' Yes.

"Then I'd always finish by asking, 'Do you want a hug from me?' Sometimes, even though I'd just given you a whole bunch of hugs from everyone else, you'd shake your head no; you didn't want a hug from me. I got a kick out of that. But you were always so emotionally open and honest. I never had to wonder how you were feeling.

"Something else I've never forgotten about you happened the day of one of your surgeries. There were so many I don't remember which one. But the day before, I'd tried to prepare you by explaining what was going to happen in the morning. That when you woke up you would be hungry, but that we couldn't give you a bottle or anything to eat until after the doctors took you into the other room.

"The surgery was scheduled for eight o'clock in the morning, so you weren't allowed to ingest anything after midnight. Naturally you were hungry when you woke up the next morning, and you asked for a bottle. So I reminded you of what we'd talked about the day before—how you would just have to be hungry until the doctors came and took you into the other room. That it would just be a little while to wait.

"But something went wrong that morning. There were a couple other surgical cases before yours, and they didn't go as planned. Or there was some kind of emergency. Because nine o'clock came and went. Ten. Eleven. Noon. One o'clock. I tried to distract you by racing you up and down the hall in a wheelchair. We played games. I knew you were hungry. If we'd have known you weren't going to get into the OR until four in the afternoon, you could have had something. Yet after I explained in the morning that you would have to wait to eat or drink anything, you never asked again.

"Most adult patients would have been begging for something. And at two years of age you shouldn't have had the ability to remember and process that kind of abstract thought. Yet somehow you did. And that amazed me. Your very survival amazed everyone else."

Getting out of the tent meant that everyone would finally get an up close look at the new me. Until then, when Mom helped give me a bath, not even my parents had gotten a clear look at the extent of the damage to my body.

"He may be changed on the outside. But he's the same Joel on the inside."

I looked different. So different that my parents worried about how Jami would react when she saw me clearly outside the tent for the first time. They told her, "Because Joel was burned, he looks different now. His skin is redder. It looks and even feels different now. We have these pictures to show you. And if you have any questions, we'll try to answer them."

Jami picked up the photographs and stared at them for a little while. Then she put them down and said, "He may be changed on the outside. But he's the same Joel on the inside."

As far as my four-year-old sister was concerned, that was that. Unfortunately, I would soon learn that not everyone had such an insightful reaction.

C h a p t e r   5

On Groundhog's Day 1980 the Shriners Burn Institute in Boston finally released me to go home for the first time since the accident. I have no idea whether or not Puxatawney Phil saw his shadow that morning. But my own four-and-a-half-month confinement was finally over. And I'm sure things looked brighter for my entire family.

I don't remember arriving home in Nyack. I'd been gone so long and had so much medicine in me that I'm not sure I realized we were home. Or even what home meant anymore. My parents tell me they carried me from room to room, trying to trigger some recollection in my two-year-old mind that "this is your room; those are your toys; we're home, Joel!"

As thrilled as we all must have felt to be living together as a family again in our own house, most days it seemed as though we'd brought the hospital home with us. I was still a critically injured burn patient. Every day the entire family's life revolved around my needs and the continuing challenge of my ongoing medical care. It had to. My life depended on it.

Just changing the dressings on my various wounds could take the better part of an hour—sometimes longer. And they had to be changed up to four times a day in the beginning.

Even though she was trained as a nurse, there was no way Mom could begin to care for all my physical needs and still do everything else required of a young wife and mother. As much as she wanted to. And as much as she tried to.

Fortunately, a number of family friends and wives of Nyack students were nurses willing to help. So Mom set up a regular schedule of daily care that included five nurses every week.

Each morning, soon after dawn, one of the volunteer nurses would let herself into the house and slip into my room to begin my daily routine. If her arrival didn't awaken the rest of the household, I soon would—because as soon as I opened my eyes and saw the nurse, I began to scream. Thankfully, I don't remember a lot of details from that time, but I do vividly recall the sound of my own screams.

In order to better understand and describe what I went through, I recently watched a video of just one of the hundreds of dressing changes that took place in those first weeks after I came home from the hospital. Rather, I viewed part of a video—until I didn't want to see or hear any more of it. I didn't need to watch the entire video; I'd already lived it.

I screamed continuously as the nurse slowly unwrapped each arm and each leg to remove the leg splints I wore every night. I screamed as she rubbed cream over the recent skin grafts, still angry and red, that nearly covered my entire body. But I started screaming loudest of all at the very first indication it was time to begin changing the dressing on my skull.

There was so much gauze and tape wrapped around my head that the protective helmet I wore whenever I got out of bed had to be nearly big enough to fit a basketball. And since that wrapping almost always stuck to the open wound on top of my head, the removal of the wrapping seemed more like medieval torture than modern medical procedure. Fast or slow, there was no pleasant way to peel off the sterile pads and bandages. The burned area, which encompassed nearly the entire top of my head, had to be cleaned with a regimen of rinses— including saline solution, hydrogen peroxide, and silver nitrate. Fresh, sterile, dry pads were applied to the wound and then bound tightly in place with more gauze and tape.

Watching the old video it was clear that this procedure, which had to be repeated two to four times each day, was a horrific one. But what made it so difficult for me to watch wasn't so much the obvious pain I had to endure; I have only vague memories of the pain. What bothered me most about that videotape was reliving the maddening sense of helplessness. Those recorded screams were not so much a response to the pain as they were my only means of expressing frustration. I wasn't old enough to verbalize my deepest emotions any other way. And when the video showed me sitting in a crib, being unwrapped and wrapped against my will, deep within my soul was triggered an intensity of feeling—anger, helplessness, and frustration.

That's why I screamed. That's what I remember.

As a nurse, Mom initially wanted to be involved with the dressing changes and provide all the rest of my physical care. But with Dad's encouragement—perhaps at his insistence—she began to let the nurses do whatever they could. My parents still had to plan schedules, train new nurses, and supervise all my care. And there were still many times when Mom and Dad had to be the bad guys—the ones who subjected me to the pain and frustration of unpleasant yet necessary physical care. But more often than not they tried to assume the roles of comforter and encourager, so that most of the time when I reached the end of an hour-long dressing change and screaming match, I wanted nothing more than to throw my arms around my mother's neck and get my recommended daily allowance of affection.

I was the quintessential "high maintenance" kid. Dressing changes were merely the beginning.

The steady stream of surgical supplies coming into the house must have seemed overwhelming. Mom ordered, stored, and maintained a running inventory that showed how many boxes (and sometimes cases) there were on hand of sterile and nonsterile gloves, Ace bandages, safety pins, splints, various sizes of gauze, emollient creams, sterile salt water, peroxide, silver nitrate, other medicines, and assorted tapes.

A lot of days there seemed to be even more going out than coming in. Dad would haul up to thirty-five big bags of garbage to the curb every week on trash day. Most of it consisted of used medical supplies.

On the one hand the Sonnenberg house had been transformed into a hospital. And yet it still needed to be a home—not just for me but for my parents and my sister, Jami, who'd "lost" her entire family for most of those months following the accident.

I had survived with some of the worst burn injuries in history. And I had only begun to recover. So I still needed to be treated like a patient, which made it difficult for the rest of the family to get on with life and return to their own routine. Indeed, our family routine would never again be the same.

Fortunately, Dad is a master coordinator. He always has a plan. He and Mom started training the volunteer nurses right away. They made a list of all the necessary treatments. The nurses were all instructed to chart their procedures and observations in a notebook that was kept in the closet along with all the supplies.

Still, nothing came easily. Even feeding me became a major challenge. The burn scars went so deep in my cheeks and face that my jaws would barely open. Which made it difficult to even get food in my mouth. A spoon wouldn't fit.

To make matters worse, I now required a high-protein diet to replenish what few muscles I had left. Plus, I needed supplements of extra vitamins and calories added to my milk bottles in order to gain strength and weight. On top of that, I had always been one hungry kid.

So mealtimes became a daily challenge that required both creativity and endurance. My parents would have to cut or tear food into itty-bitty pieces and poke them through my tiny mouth opening and place them in the top and back of my mouth with their fingertips. Even something as small as an M&M had to be squashed flatter in order to get it in.

Nutrition was only one of the challenges my folks faced. They were just as concerned about mobility. I'd been walking for several months at the time the accident happened. But I'd spent almost six months since then in a hospital bed. And I no longer had any toes. Would I be able to learn to walk again?

A physical therapist agreed to come to the house, which meant we saved time and energy in not having to venture out for that treatment. While it simplified the family schedule, it didn't make things easy. I screamed every time the therapist walked in the door. And I screamed pretty much continuously throughout every therapy session.

I don't think this response had much to do with pain either. For a time I routinely screamed whenever a strange adult walked into the house and began to approach me. Not only nurses and therapists, but family friends. Experience in the hospital and now even at home had taught me that most adults had plans for me. Their plans took precedent, no matter how I felt about the issue. And the fact that I had no control or say-so both frustrated and infuriated me. Every day, every person was a battle. So I protested the only way I knew how.

I also screamed and kicked the sides of the crib with my splints whenever I awakened. Which happened four to six times almost every night.

Mom now admits there were times my screaming went on for so long she thought she was going to lose her mind. Some days the lack of sleep and the nearly endless crying ratcheted up the household tension to the point where everyone wanted to scream. But other days the constant auditory stimulation worked more like a mind-numbing drug.

Mom says there were times friends would call, and when she answered the phone, they would want to know what in the world was wrong. "What do you mean?" she'd ask.

"That noise that sounds like screaming," they'd say.

"Oh, that's just Joel," she'd tell them.

"Is he all right? Do you need to go check on him?"

"He's fine," she'd assure the caller. "He's just getting his dressings changed." If they only knew.

A lot of people sensed enough to be very concerned about our whole family's emotional health. And a surprising number of them cared enough to offer all kinds of love and concern and some very practical support. Friends regularly provided meals. One woman came to wash dishes, do laundry, and clean the house a couple times a week to free Mom up to spend more time with me and with Jami. Another volunteered her secretarial skills to help deal with the flood of correspondence our family was receiving.

My scars and grafts were so tender and irritable I had to wear 100 percent cotton clothes—because cotton is cooler and breathes better than other fabric. So people made me special outfits—overalls, shirts, even pajamas. One woman designed and made customized T-shirts with Velcro fasteners in the back to solve the problem of pulling the shirts on over my heavily bandaged head.

Nyack College continued to pay Dad's salary, even though he wasn't there to teach. But people at church knew our family was facing heavy financial burdens during this time. They also knew there was no way either of my parents could afford the time or energy to pursue an additional part-time job. So a group of friends banded together, pooled their resources, and provided us with an additional regular monthly income my parents could count on for as long as they needed it—as much or more money than my folks could have earned with a second job.

But of all the thoughtful and generous things people did for our family during that difficult time, my mom and dad say what they felt and appreciated the most were the prayers, the concerns, and the encouragement expressed by so many friends, loved ones, and even complete strangers. My parents needed that. Our whole family needed that. Because our ordeal was far from over.

When my folks had finally brought me home from the hospital that February day, they knew we'd have to go back for many more procedures. And the first return visit came all too soon.

Around Memorial Day we drove back to the hospital in Boston for yet another operation. This time the plastic surgeon worked on the thick scar that was my upper lip—to loosen it up and also to widen my mouth at the corners to make it easier for me to eat. For several days after the surgery I couldn't eat anything; I was fed through a tube. And I had to stay in the hospital for more than two weeks before they let me go home.

I have very few specific memories from the long hospitalization right after the accident. I was a little too young. And some of the details from that first return visit may also be all jumbled up with countless vague recollections from the many more subsequent hospitalizations yet to come. However, it's very possible that one of my very earliest and distinct childhood memories took place that spring in Boston, during the time I was back at Shriners.

I remember a specific dressing change.

One of the hospital nurses hurriedly unwrapped my arms and legs. Both her speed and the way she avoided eye contact were bad signs of things to come.

Back home, the volunteer nurses and my parents took their time and tried to be as careful as possible. Sometimes when the bandage or one of the sterile pads had crusted dry and got really stuck in a wound, they would put me in the bathtub and soak it loose painlessly.

Hospital nurses never did that. They would have had to reserve a tub ahead of time without knowing if they really needed it. Plus, they simply didn't have that much time to devote to one patient.

Okay, maybe there is less pain when you yank off a bandage in a split second than if you spend a long minute trying to carefully peel it free from a scabby wound. But the sudden-jerk technique certainly seemed a lot scarier to me at the age of two and a half.

That's what this vivid childhood memory was all about.

The nurse changing my dressings that day was undoubtedly in a big hurry. I clung tightly to her arms as she began to unwrap my arms and legs; I'd learned that this was the only way of slowing the nurses down and trying to control the pain. Still, this nurse worked fast and none too carefully. I was so frightened as she started on the bandage around my head that I cringed. And I clearly remember pleading with her, "Be gentle! Please be gentle!"

She wasn't. At least she wasn't as gentle as I wanted her to be. Nor was she as gentle as Mom and my home care nurses at Nyack were. As unpleasant as dressing changes were at home, it seemed like nothing compared to the utter helplessness I experienced at the hospital when nothing I said or did made any difference. That's why I screamed so much.

I know I owe a lot to the Shriners and their Boston burn center. They saved my life. They provided hundreds of thousands of dollars worth of care for free. And we met many caring people who worked there. But it was still a hospital, and their job was to get me home.

I quickly realized home was better. And that gave me all the reason I needed to decide I absolutely despised hospitals—which was not a good thing, considering how many more hospital visits still loomed in my future.

Thankfully, the surgery succeeded in making it easier for my parents to feed me. They could at least get a spoon in my mouth.

There were other encouraging indications of progress that spring as well. Not only had I learned to walk again, but I soon began running everywhere I went. With the return of my full-speed-ahead personality, I really needed that hard plastic helmet the doctors said I'd have to wear to protect the top of my head for years—maybe even for the rest of my life.

But as the other wounds healed and I became stronger and more mobile, my world literally expanded. With a lessened chance of injuries and infections, I was finally allowed to go outdoors to play on the porch or in the sandbox with my sister.

My parents tried to explain to Jami in four-year-old terms that even though I looked different, they wanted me to be able to do as many things as I could for myself. That even though I no longer had hands and fingers, I could still play if I learned to pick things up with my wrists. So right away, like the big sister she was, Jami began mothering and teaching me by showing me what to do: "Pick it up this way, Joel." My sister may have done almost as much as my parents did to prepare me for reintegration into the world.

Here again, wonderful family friends, the Nyack College community, and the folks at our local church made a huge difference. Dad took me on hikes, just as he'd promised to do on the tape he made for me two days after I was burned. I loved traipsing all over campus, perched high on Dad's shoulders, my bandaged, overall-covered legs dangling around his neck. Everyone we met seemed to smile and wave as they greeted me: "Hi, Joel." It was great.

What wasn't so great was the reaction some kids had when they first saw me. Like the time Dad and I were out walking and I saw my friend John playing in his yard. He had known me since we were six months old and could sit up and play together in our sandboxes and plastic kiddie pools.

I knew John saw Dad and me coming, because he was staring right at us. But when we got closer, he got frightened and ran into his house. Sometimes even older kids who'd known and played with me since I was a baby would walk past me without speaking or even looking at me.

Another of my best friends at church, a boy named Ryan, began to cry every time he looked at me. It went on for weeks. My parents went to his parents to ask if there was anything they could do to help. Ryan's parents were embarrassed; the other kids were accepting me back as part of the group.

No one knew what to do about Ryan. Until one Sunday Ryan went home so excited. He told his mother, "Mom, Mom, guess what? I touched Joel. I touched Joel, Mom. And I didn't get burned!" All that time he'd thought I was on fire and that if he touched me, he would be burned as badly as I was.

From then on Ryan and I were friends again.

Lots of families at church reached out to us. Their love and acceptance made me feel welcome there. It gave my parents the strength and encouragement they needed to endure other tough times and other people who proved far less sensitive.

As a two-and-a-half-year-old I still had a very limited understanding of what was going on. Just as I noticed how everyone around campus seemed to know who I was and say "Hi, Joel" whenever I went on walks with my dad, I couldn't help realizing that people often stared at me whenever Mom or Dad took me out in public.

When I eventually learned why, my parents tried to reassure me by saying, "People just don't understand. If they knew you like we do, Joel, they would love you too."

It wasn't until much later that I learned about some of the most insensitive situations and people my parents endured. Like the man who asked Dad, "Is that thing yours?" Or the grocery store cashier who checked Mom out, and after we walked away had muttered, "Why do they bring that child out in public? What a disgrace!" Or the time Dad and I were at a playground and two laughing teenage boys egged their little brother into coming over and asking, "What's a monkey doing sliding down this slide?"

Insensitivity and discrimination would become just part of life for me and my family. But we certainly didn't dwell on it. As a young child I didn't understand or even notice some of it. And my parents sheltered me as much as possible from the worst of the cruelty.

But they knew, as I would soon find out, that they wouldn't be able to protect me forever.

C h a p t e r   6

That spring the doctors informed my parents that the open wound on the top of my head, where my badly burned skull had remained exposed, looked as though it would eventually heal. They expected granulation tissues (scar tissue) to gradually grow over the affected area. And if the skin growing in from the edges didn't eventually cover the wound, they should be able to graft skin over it. In the meantime we'd just have to wait and see what happened.

They did say they expected the skull itself to continue growing throughout my life. While it would probably be only half the thickness it should have been, they didn't think I'd need to have a metal plate installed. Nor did they think I'd need to wear my helmet once the exposed skull was covered with skin.

Of course, I was too young to understand all the implications of this prognosis. But my parents were so thrilled that they sent out a letter to family, friends, and lots of other people who'd been praying for me to say they were "relieved at this news and praising God."

The letter went on to give a medical update and explain:

The major problems the doctors see are with Joel's face and hands. Surgical procedures performed on Joel's face will primarily be functional, not cosmetic, in nature. There is little that will or can be done for his face cosmetically due to the lack of unburned skin on Joel's body that can be used for grafts.

Joel will need continual releases of the scar tissue on his body throughout his growing years. When scar tissue contracts, it pulls on the surrounding skin and renders some body parts nonfunctioning unless it is cut into to allow for movement. Particularly affected are the mouth, eyes, neck, shoulders, and underarm areas.

Joel's left arm will eventually be fitted with a prosthesis. His right hand will need to be operated on—probably about the time he starts school—to create a pincer movement. . . . Please pray!

Not only would each new proposed procedure require a trip back to Shriners, but in between operations we had to return to Boston for follow-up care, routine exams, and conferences with the medical team to discuss plans for additional upcoming treatments. Not only did all those trips present an exhausting physical challenge for our family, they were fast becoming a serious financial drain. Driving the ten-hour round trip (the cheapest way to go) consumed the most time and emotional energy—two commodities our family needed to conserve. Flying would reduce time and hassle, but the financial cost made it seem out of the question. Especially when you added in the price of lodging, meals, and city transportation while staying in Boston.

As much as they hated to do it, my parents decided they had no choice but to ask for help. They took me into New York City for an appointment with the head of a large philanthropic organization known for providing financial assistance to families with medical needs. But the man who met with us wasn't the least bit sympathetic. He brusquely informed my parents there was no money available for them to stay with me in Boston. "Why don't you just take him to the hospital and leave him there?" he wanted to know. "What's he doing out of the hospital anyway?"

Mom and Dad had felt awkward enough walking into the meeting; they felt absolutely humiliated by the time they left. They didn't know whether they were more discouraged or angered by the way we were treated. They resented the implication that there was something unreasonable about parents wanting to be with a two-year-old who was facing surgery.

But no sooner did we get home than the phone rang. The man on the line said, "Mrs. Sonnenberg, this is Jim Blake. I'm with the Rockland County Volunteer Fire Department. We heard that your son was severely burned, and we wondered if there was anything we could do to be of assistance to your family."

Mom told him she couldn't believe the timing of his call. She explained what had happened during the appointment that morning. Mr. Blake said the local fire department would be glad to help. And the Rockland County Volunteer Fire Department generously paid our airfare to Boston and back from that time on.

The generosity of concerned people, many of them complete strangers, continued to surprise us all. It provided our family with an experience that became for all of us the highlight of 1980 and many other years yet to come.

Good friends who were convinced that our family needed a break from the grueling daily routine invited us to spend a week with them at CAMP-of-the-WOODS, a Christian retreat center in the Adirondack Mountains of upstate New York. When my parents contacted the camp to make reservations, they were informed that the week they wanted to come was already full. But our friends had briefed the administration there about us. So the Purdy family, who ran the camp, told us to come anyway. That if the Lord meant for us to be there, something would open up.

So my parents packed the car and headed north. But not without thinking about what happened the last time they'd planned a family vacation—less than a year before.

Sure enough. Something did "open up" for us at CAMP-of-the-WOODS. Only the best accommodations in the whole place. At no charge. The owners refused to let us pay anything. And the afternoon prior to our arrival, the Purdys informed their 200-member camp staff we were coming. "This family has been through a very tragic experience." They summarized our story. "These people are physically and emotionally exhausted. So we want every staff member to go out of his or her way to make sure they feel special. Give them the red-carpet treatment. In the dining hall, at the snack shop, on the beach. We want you bending over backward for these people. When they leave here, we want them to feel emotionally, physically, and spiritually renewed. We want you all to feel responsible for making this a great week for the Sonnenberg family."

And it was.

Word evidently went around the entire camp about me. Everywhere we went all week, people would say, "Hi, Joel, how are you?" or "Joel, my name is _____, and I think you're special!" Most people simply accepted us without my parents having to explain to everyone what had happened to me.

The Purdys and their camp staff gave me the royal treatment. They took us on boat rides and let me "steer." It was every kid's dream come true. The assistant camp director also let me "drive" his souped-up jeep. We swam. We sailboated.

Mom and Dad went waterskiing. And after we kids got to sleep at night, the camp provided babysitters so my parents could attend evening events or go out to nearby restaurants alone.

During our last evening meal in the camp dining hall, staff members with trumpets and trombones surrounded our table. Dad hoisted me onto his shoulders and began to bob up and down to the beat as the music played, and the other diners began to clap along and sing:

> For he's a jolly good fellow,
> For he's a jolly good fellow,
> For he's a jolly good fellow,
> Which nobody can deny.

As they serenaded me I laughed, swooping up and down on my father's shoulders, my bandaged arms spread like the wings of a plane—flying above the crowd. I guess people all around that big dining room were crying. But I didn't notice. I was too busy enjoying the end of my best week ever.

Our stay at CAMP-of-the-WOODS offered a cool respite from medical treatments and an otherwise long, hot summer. Because my newly grafted skin was very sensitive to intensive ultraviolet rays, I needed to stay out of the sun from about eleven in the morning to about three every afternoon. Even so, something caused my skin to break out in a miserable rash at all my graft sites. I'd be awakened almost every summer night by the itching and the heat. It took almost the entire summer to figure out that what had caused my misery was an allergic reaction to lanolin in the skin cream the nurses had applied to my arms and legs and body every day. As soon as we switched creams, the rash went away.

Unfortunately, not all of my physical challenges were so quickly and simply remedied. I was becoming more aware of my facial disfigurement. I didn't look like Jami—or like anyone else I saw when I looked around me. But what bothered me most was when I'd be playing and realize I couldn't manipulate objects as easily as my friends could.

"No fingers. Can't do!" became my frequent cry of frustration. Maybe that's one reason the doctors moved up their timetable for working on my hand.

In September of 1980, almost exactly a year after the accident, I went back to Boston for the first and worst step in a complicated series of medical procedures designed to give me some functional use of my right hand. My parents tried to explain what was going to happen and why. But there was no way it could all sink into my not-quite-three-year-old mind. *The doctors said they were going to help me. How come whenever they said that, they always had to hurt me first?* I couldn't even move my arm for six weeks.

They referred to the procedure as a "groin flap." The idea was to transfer a big chunk of skin and tissue from my unburned upper leg to the end of my right arm to make for me a full-sized hand in the place where all the fingers had been burned off. And the first step of the process was to cut deep incisions in the groin area of my leg to free the "flap," insert what remained of my right hand into the open wound, and then sew shut the flap of healthy skin and tissue around it. As the "groin flap" and the rest of my hand began to heal together, the doctors gradually began to slice the flap away from my leg.

Throughout this process the medical staff tried to keep me distracted and busy with physical therapy and play therapy. But there was no way any active preschooler could ignore having his arm sewn into his leg for six weeks.

My parents tried to stay with me at the hospital whenever they could. But sometimes one or both of them had to go home. And they never were allowed to spend the night in my hospital room—which sometimes bothered my mother a lot.

"Joel, do you ever wake up in the middle of the night in the hospital?" she asked.

I nodded.

"What do you do then? Do you cry? Why do you wake up?"

"Too noisy," I told her.

"What do you do? Do you tell them to be quiet?"

"No. Just sit."

"Do you go back to sleep?"

"This is very important, Joel. Jesus is always with you. Always."

I nodded. "Sometimes." I did have a special blanket and a stuffed dog named Fluffy who stayed with me when my parents couldn't.

"Joel, I want you to remember something," my mother told me. I nodded and listened to her say, "This is very important, Joel. Jesus is always with you. Always. He is with you, just like Fluffy is. He's right there beside you. He is very strong— even stronger than Daddy. He knows what is best and will always be there."

When I finally went home again, my "new" hand didn't seem any better than what I'd had before. It didn't even look like other people's hands. It seemed awfully big and floppy on the end of my skinny arm. More like a paw or the big part of a mitten, with another loose flap of skin on the side. "That's where they're going to put a bone to make you a thumb," my parents tried to explain.

"No fingers?" I still had to pick things up by using my two wrists.

"Next time you come to the hospital they're going to put a bone in to give you a thumb. Then you'll be able to do all kinds of things!" my parents assured me.

That part sounded good. But I didn't ever want to see the hospital again.

There was much for our family to be grateful for that Thanksgiving of 1980. And our local newspaper, the *Rockland Journal News*, summed it up in an article headlined "Family of Burned Child Counts Holiday Blessings":

> He scampers about his house with the vigor of robust health and the excitement of restless youth. His bright eyes size you up from beneath his bandages, and determine whether you are a trustworthy friend or an ignorant fool. He has known many of both.
>
> He good-humoredly maneuvers his stubbed-off arms to hold a glass of milk to his immobile lips, and when you ask him how old he is now, he answers with an ear-shattering, "THREE!"
>
> His name is Joel Sonnenberg, and Thanksgiving, important as it is to all Americans, has a special meaning to him and his family.
>
> Last year Joel was severely burned in a car crash in Hampton, N.H., ... when a truck plowed full speed into a string of cars waiting at a toll plaza. Joel was not expected to live.
>
> Last year, his parents, Mike and Janet, of South Nyack, felt extremely grateful that their son was alive to see Thanksgiving. He had sustained the worst burns of any survivor in medical history, had already undergone more than a dozen operations, and was confined to a plastic tent in a Boston hospital.
>
> In the crash, most of Joel's skin was burned off, as were his fingers, toes, ears, and nose. He was left with a hole in his skull and must wear a ... helmet most of the time.
>
> But this year, the Sonnenbergs' blessings have multiplied. Today, the boy who was lucky just to breathe [last year] is alert, healthy, and strong. Though badly disfigured, he's learning the lessons of life: talking, eating, playing, and socializing with other youngsters, most of them neighbors from the Nyack College community where his father teaches biology. He's being prepared through the devotion of parents and the

kindness of strangers for a life as normal as possible. And it seems the closer Joel's life gets to normal, the farther from it his parents' lives get. That's a problem they're grateful to have.*

The article went on to talk about all the volunteers who provided help with the nursing and housework. It cited the local fire department paying our transportation to and from Boston, the wonderful CAMP-of-the-WOODS experience, and all the free medical care provided at the Shriners Burn Institute in Boston.

The newspaper told about plans to give me a thumb in the future. And then the article ended by talking about how my experience had impacted the rest of my family:

Everyone in the family has a different life because of Joel. His sister, Jami, in kindergarten at Valley Cottage School, fights for attention in her own right and generally wins.

Janet, who was seeking her second master's degree in nursing and hoping to teach it, has had to put her craft to work full-time in her own home, taking care of Joel. Unhurt in the crash, she is now expecting the Sonnenbergs' third child.

Mike was [burned] and partially paralyzed for a few months after the accident, but he said he has recovered completely. He, however, has had to give up his pursuit of a doctorate to accompany Joel on the many trips back and forth to Boston.

"Our goals have changed," Janet said. "These career goals are somewhat superficial goals. To me, happiness, without trying to sound lofty, really depends on a right relationship with your Creator, knowing who you are and your accountability in life," she said.

"Whether you're handicapped, as Joel is, or you have everything you should have, it's how you use it. Joel can still glorify God as well as anyone else."

Many more good things happened and more milestones were reached during 1981. I started preschool classes at the local YMCA in January—another big step out into the world. Naturally, my parents were concerned about the reaction of

---

*"Family of Burned Child Counts Holiday Blessings," *Journal News*, November 27, 1980. Copyright © *The Journal News*. Reprinted with permission.

my classmates and their families. So when the teacher suggested they write a letter to the other parents even before I began to attend, that's what they did.

You might call it a letter of introduction. It told a little about what had happened to me. And then it noted, "Now Joel's needs are similar to other children's needs. It is important for him to play together with other children, to sharpen his social skills and begin his life as a vital and contributing member of our community. Just as you and your child need love and acceptance from others to maintain your self-worth, so does Joel."

That letter worked. Not only was I accepted at the school by my classmates and their parents, but before long I had many new friends whose parents and families became friends with the Sonnenberg clan.

And our clan was growing. On January 22 Mom delivered to Jami and me a new baby sister named Sommer Leigh. We'd been looking forward to the day for months—excitedly collecting favorite toys to give as gifts for our new sibling from the time our folks had told us about the expected baby.

Mom's responsibility for a brand-new baby meant Dad was elected to accompany me to Boston for the next operation on my right hand—the bone graft to give me a thumb. My parents started preparing me for it a couple weeks ahead of time.

"You and Daddy are going on an airplane again, Joel. That will be fun. You'll get to see all your old friends at the hospital in Boston. You'll get lots of treats. And the doctors will give you a new thumb!"

"Hurt?" I asked, sure there had to be a catch.

"Yes, but you'll have a new thumb and be able to do so many more things."

I remembered my last hospital stay. I began to cry.

Dad and I got up in time to catch an early-morning flight to Boston on March 18. As Mom fed me my breakfast of cereal, toast, and juice, I begged her, "No operation!"

She looked like she wanted to cry too. "I know it will hurt, honey. But Daddy will be there when you wake up. Don't forget you'll have special treats on the plane too. There will be a surprise in Daddy's pocket." When Mom said goodbye, she asked for extra kisses to give Jami and Sommer when they woke up. And even after I walked out the door with my father, I turned around and ran back inside to give her an extra bear hug.

"I love you, Mommy," I said. "I miss you."

Two days later Dad called Mom to say, "I have bad news, honey. They had to stop in the middle of Joel's surgery. He started running a high fever. He's in intensive care now, and they're running all kinds of tests. It might be a reaction to the anesthesia. But he needs prayer."

I recovered, and three days later they operated again. This time everything went smoothly. The doctors removed a bone from the palm of my hand, grafted it in the place where my thumb had been, and wrapped around it the loose piece of skin from the last surgery.

A week later I flew home with one of the strangest casts ever seen. All my clothes had to be altered to accommodate this monstrosity that went from my shoulder all the way down the arm and ended with a round sphere that made it look like I'd jammed my arm into a small bowling ball before they plastered it up.

My parents managed to think of creative ways to keep my spirits up. As Easter approached they laughingly likened the big ball at the end of my cast to a huge Easter egg that would soon be broken open to find a wonderful surprise: my new thumb.

The week before Easter we were all sitting on the couch having family time before going to bed. Tomorrow was the big day. We were going back to Boston to get my cast off. Everyone was excited, and Dad began teasing me: "Joel! I think I hear something. A little voice is coming out of your cast. What's it saying?"

I laughed and played along. "It's my thumb. It says, 'Get me out fast.'" We started talking about my hand.

"Tomorrow you'll finally get to see your thumb, Joel!"

"FINGERS!" I shouted.

"Finger," my parents corrected me.

"Five fingers!"

"No, son," Dad told me. "One thumb."

"Not five fingers? Daddy, Mommy, and Jami have five fingers."

"The doctors are giving you a very special thumb, Joel. It will help you pick up and hold things."

I began to cry and say over and over, "Me want five fingers. Me want five fingers."

Dad hugged me tight and told me, "You will have five fingers in heaven someday, Joel. Jesus promised." I think we all cried.

The next day was a great day anyway. The cast came off, and we went right from the hospital to the MacKenzies' house in New Hampshire to celebrate with a special party where we sang "Happy Birthday" for my thumb. I got to show off my new grip by using a knife to cut the cake Nancy had decorated with my favorite superhero—the Incredible Hulk.

On Easter, back in Nyack, we went to some friends' house for dinner. Jami and I were playing in their front yard when some kids we didn't know walked up. "You're disgusting!" one of them told me. "You're ugly," the other one said. When I started to cry, Jami ran inside, calling, "Mommy, Daddy, some boys are being naughty to Joel."

A few days later Jami and I were riding our Big Wheels on the sidewalk in front of our own house when a couple of kids walking by spotted me, screamed, and ran away.

The very same day a couple of older kids were walking by as we got out of our car in the driveway. One of them saw me and asked the other one, "Why does that kid wear a monster mask? Why doesn't he take it off?"

When we went out to the grocery store, I noticed many startled looks. Some folks smiled at me and were nice. But a lot of people just whispered and stared. Mom told me that when people stared at me, I should speak to them and say, "Hi, I'm Joel. What's your name?"

Sometimes the person would smile back and talk to me. Other times he or she would turn away. My family and friends and medical team were trying their best to prepare me to go out in the world. But I was about to learn that not all the world was prepared for me.

Chapter 7

My life was one of constant change and adjustment. Even the positive developments—like my new thumb—often took time to adjust to. As anxious and excited as I'd been to see my thumb during the long wait to get the cast off, I was for a time reluctant to use it.

I don't remember why. I don't think I was afraid of hurting it. I suspect it just didn't feel natural to me. I'd gotten amazingly proficient at picking up and playing with toys by gripping them between my right wrist and the end of my left arm. Any small-motor skill that required fingers to do I just let my parents or Jami handle.

My parents and my therapists made me practice picking things up with my new thumb. But outside of therapy, and when nobody was there to insist on it, I used my wrists or asked for help. Which frustrated my parents no end.

"Try to do it with your thumb, Joel," they'd say.

I'd think, *Why?* and do it the way I'd already learned to cope.

Until the Fourth of July. After supper my parents broke out a box of sparklers. They lit one and handed it to Jami, who waved it around as everyone cheered. I'd never seen sparklers, so I was entranced.

When Jami's sparkler fizzled out, Dad lit another one and gave it to her. She waved it around to more oohs and aahs. It looked like so much fun that I wanted one of my own.

"You can't have one unless you use your thumb, Joel. To be safe you have to hold it with your thumb."

"Okay!" I said. The payoff looked as though it'd be worth it.

Dad lit the next sparkler and carefully handed it to me so that I could grip the bare part of the wire between my thumb and hand. I waved it around and

59

made patterns in the air. When it burned out, I got another. And another. Until all the sparklers were gone.

Then we went back into the house and had strawberry shortcake for dessert. Without any coaxing I picked up my spoon, holding it between my thumb and hand. And then I tried to feed myself.

From that night on I began to find more and more uses for my new thumb. And more than a few new rewards.

I was too young to fully understand how closely my parents worked and consulted with my teachers. But together they made preschool one of the true highlights of my life by ensuring that I continued to be accepted by the other students and their parents.

I quickly developed a bunch of friends—guys and girls—who treated me like everyone else. We not only worked and played together in the classroom and out on the playground, but we regularly spent time in each other's homes after school and on weekends. Unlike the many strangers whose stares made it impossible to forget I was different, my friends soon accepted me for who I am: Joel.

Sure, I knew I was different. And I think, even then, part of me understood I always would be. Where a lot of kids try to bolster their self-identity by dressing or behaving in such a way as to draw attention to themselves, I never had to resort to that. Rather, I desperately wanted to be as much like everyone else as I could possibly be, and to do whatever they did.

I guess that's why I resisted anything and everything that emphasized or called attention to the differences. Even those things that were supposed to make my life easier.

For example, feeding myself continued to be a challenge. Not only did my mouth present a small target, but getting food and drink in there was doubly difficult without fingers. Letting my parents feed me was the simplest and most efficient solution at home. But they couldn't go to school with me every day, and I wouldn't have wanted them to. Which meant I needed to become independent at the table.

My rehabilitation therapists tried to help. They provided me with a special cup that looked and worked a lot like those sippy cups babies drink from. But I wasn't a baby, so I refused to use it. They also tried strapping silverware to the end of my left arm, but I didn't like that either. I didn't want to do or use anything that would make me seem more different than I already was. So I kept working at maneuvering a spoon or a fork with my right hand. It wasn't ever pretty, and it was seldom very efficient. I would always have trouble cutting anything harder than a noodle. But I eventually managed to make do at mealtimes.

Other activities proved to be just too much of a challenge. Arts and crafts projects were good examples. I had a specially designed pair of scissors that worked okay for cutting a sheet of paper on a desk. But holding up a piece of paper and cutting out some special shape—like a star or a handprint—was simply impossible for me.

So it was that my teachers gave me extra help during arts and crafts time. Which wasn't all bad. You know how teachers always have a demonstration model to show students ahead of time, so they can say, "This is how it's supposed to look." When they'd say that, I remember thinking, *That's how mine IS gonna look. Everyone else's is going to look like slop.* Sometimes there were advantages to needing and getting expert help.

However, I didn't have the same positive attitude about the prosthesis designed for me. The doctors had to cut back some of the bone in my left arm and smooth out the stump so that the prosthesis could fit over it and be strapped around my shoulder. At the end of this artificial arm, in place of a hand, was a rather ominous and impressive hook. By flexing my left shoulder, I could open and close the parallel halves of the hook in a sort of sideways pincher motion.

It didn't exactly make me ambidextrous, but the hook certainly doubled my capacity to grasp and manipulate things. I remember putting the hook to good use right away by hoisting and moving plastic toy soldiers around my imaginary battlefield. But the novelty soon wore off, and I quit wanting to wear the contraption.

Here, too, part of the problem was my not wanting to call attention to my injuries. My parents must have understood that because they enlisted my friends to encourage me to wear the hook. They begged me to wear it to school; everyone wanted to see how I made the thing work. It actually seemed as though they envied my special appendage.

It was a wicked-looking weapon. So I admit there was a perverse sort of appeal that most boys could probably relate to. It gave me a sense of special power to think, *Nobody better mess with me!* I knew if I ever got in a fight, I could have done some serious damage with that thing.

So I was eventually persuaded to give the hook a try. It worked a lot like my reconstructed right hand. Both utilized a practical, yet limited, pinching motion. I could grip the edge of a glass or pick up a piece of clothing with my hook, but any activity requiring fine-motor skills—such as writing or drawing—demanded that I use my right hand. I soon learned there were also some large-motor skills that weren't well suited to my new arm.

Our house in Nyack, which sat on a steep hill, had a great yard for kids. Dad planted flower beds in the shape of each of our initials. We had a wonderful back-yard garden from which Mom made the most delicious strawberry-rhubarb pies. And in the fall we had tons of leaves, which we raked into an eight-foot-high pile that stood above the rest of the yard almost as high as our garage and drive-way were. Then we'd climb up the driveway, leap down into the pile, and liter-ally disappear in the sea of leaves. Nothing could have been more fun for kids.

Except maybe the hours I spent hiding high up in a Chinese maple that was *the* perfect climbing tree. Often I'd climb up there all alone, but sometimes I'd sit in the top branches, sharing secret adventures with my friends. When it came time to get down, my most daring buddies would descend along the trunk until they were just a few feet off the ground, then they would jump out, grab hold of one of the lower branches, let their momentum swing them out away from the tree, release their grip, and then drop softly the last three or four feet to the ground. It always looked like such a cool maneuver.

One day when I'd been up in the tree by myself, I stopped on the way down and studied the branch my friends would swing on. I felt certain I could leap out far enough to grab it with my right hand. No problem there. I examined the hook on my left arm and eyeballed the limb again. It looked small enough in diame-ter to fit in my hook if I caught it just right.

I reviewed the steps in my mind. Bend my knees. Lean away from the trunk. Leap. Stretch for the branch. Grab hold. Let the momentum swing my body out. Release. Arch my back. And drop softly to my feet on the ground below, with a landing so perfect that even the Russian judge would have to give me at least a 9.5. I can do this!

So I did. And everything worked just as I envisioned it. For a split second I was flying through the air. I caught the branch perfectly with my hand and my hook. My body swung out. At the very top of my swing I arched my back and let go with my right hand.

Suddenly I jerked to a halt in midflight. My feet swung back under me toward the tree, then out again, then in toward the tree, then out again. Back and forth I swayed in an ever-decreasing arc until I hung motionless in midair, looking past my feet to the ground just two feet below. But it may as well have been ten feet for all I could reach.

I looked back up at my hook, which seemed so far above my head that I felt like one of those action figures with the stretchable limbs. I studied the hook where it hung over the limb.

I'd gauged my jump perfectly. I'd caught the limb just the way I'd intended. I'd swung high. And I'd let go at exactly the right moment. With my right hand anyway.

The problem was obvious—all in the engineering. The hook had indeed slipped over the branch very easily. But the tip came so far down around the limb that, with my weight pulling against it, it wouldn't have slipped off unless I'd swung high enough to get my body above the branch. And if the hook slipped free at that point, chances would be good I'd land on my head and blow any chance of getting good numbers from any of the judges. So there I was, hanging from a branch by my hook, my feet stretching futilely for the ground, with no way to swing back far enough to catch the branch I'd jumped from.

So I did what I thought any would-be Olympic champion or self-respecting superhero would do in such a hapless predicament: I yelled bloody murder for help.

Mom came racing out of the house to see what was wrong and found me hanging from that Chinese maple like a lonely, lopsided Christmas tree ornament. For a split second she thought I'd somehow managed to hang myself: *After all he's survived, now he dies by hanging himself in a maple tree.* Then, quickly determining the real problem, she stepped underneath me and boosted me up to relieve just enough weight so that I could lift the hook up and off the branch. Then she lowered me to the ground, hugged me tightly, and told me in no uncertain terms that I was not to attempt that stunt ever again.

I didn't have to. There were plenty of other stunts to try. Some worked; others required similar rescues. Like another time Mom heard me screaming and came rushing outside to find me hanging upside down by my hook on our tire swing. She wasn't tall enough to get me down that time, so she had to scream for a college student across the street to come and help.

I realize now how much I must have worried my parents with such antics. But they understood how important it was for me to try to do everything my friends did. They also realized the older I got, the more aware I was becoming of the differences.

When I was just about four, I asked, "When will my skin be smooth and soft like yours, Mom?"

"You do have smooth skin, Joel," she assured me. "On your hand, your neck, and your tummy."

"But when will my arms and face be soft like yours and Sommer's?" I wanted to know.

"Because you've been burned," she said, "they probably won't be. Not until we get to heaven."

"When are we going to heaven? Tomorrow?"

"Probably not. Whenever Jesus wants us there, we'll go."

"I hope it's tomorrow."

I didn't understand all the implications. But I certainly knew that being burned made my life very different from everyone else around me. Different from my sisters. Different from my friends.

They didn't have to go back to the hospital every few months for the doctors to do more work. (By the time I was five I'd been through more than thirty surgeries.) They didn't have to play in hot and sweaty pressure garments that felt like a supertight wet suit with long underwear inside, designed to compress the scar tissue and make it smoother. They didn't have to endure the tight plastic mask or the strange-looking stints with the yellow marshmallow padding I wore after facial surgery. They didn't have to insert an uncomfortable oral splint before they went to sleep every night to keep their mouth opening from constricting any further. And they didn't have to wear a big, bulky football helmet to school.

Did I need anyone telling me I was unique and special? I don't think so.

Those things were my life. I'd never known anything else.

There probably was one thing I did wish I could change at the time. Looking back, I guess I'd say it was the single most difficult aspect of the physical ordeal for me—the ongoing care of my head wound. For nearly four years I had a raw, open wound where the fire had burned down into my skull. So every day—no less than twice a day and sometimes as many as four times a day—the dressings had to be changed.

I got so I could tell how unpleasant a changing was going to be just by watching the nurse open the package of sterile bandages. Not that it was ever what you would call pleasant. But just like watching a person tear open a Band-Aid wrapper tells you something about their experience and expertise with Band-Aids, you could tell a lot by watching a person open up a package of sterile bandages. Experience showed. And experience was usually a good thing.

After all these years I can still hear the familiar crinkling of the plastic and paper wrapping the sterile bandages came in. I will never forget that sound. I remember the vivid contrast between the clean bandages going on and the crusted filthiness of the old bandages that came off. And at least twice a day I remember the pain of gauze being torn free—like a massive Band-Aid being ripped off my head.

Perhaps it was because they had to subject me to such a horrible daily ordeal for so many months and years that my parents became so determined to help me enjoy whatever positive experience they could provide. At school. With friends. And in every normal childhood activity possible.

I played on a T-ball team with a bunch of my friends. I hit surprisingly well. I'd hold the barrel of the bat with my right hand and pin the handle tight against my body with my left arm. Then I'd twist my body around to swing the bat. I even became proficient at hitting pitched balls the same way in the backyard.

Defensive baseball skills presented a far greater challenge. I could actually catch a ball pretty well wearing a glove on my right hand. How to throw the ball once I caught it was the bigger bugaboo. I tried using a scooping motion with the glove to toss the ball, but I never could achieve any real distance or accuracy that way. My parents encouraged me to use my hook to remove the ball from my glove and throw it to the appropriate base.

Sometimes it would work. But just as often the ball would squirt out and sail in a completely different direction. Without any real fingers I couldn't grip a baseball much better with my right hand than I could with my artificial hook. Which is why I decided baseball wasn't going to be my sport and why I never played on an organized team again after T-ball.

Soccer, however, was a whole different story. Despite the doctors' early concerns about my mobility, less than a year after the accident I was running everywhere. I was as fast as (or faster than) any of my friends and classmates. And as soon as they realized I could kick a ball harder than anyone else my age, my parents helped organize a preschool soccer program at the same YMCA where I attended nursery school.

I was the star. At least I thought I was. And I loved it.

My parents watched for ways to provide me with positive and successful personal experiences in school, sports, and social relationships. But they didn't limit their goals to my immediate life and relationships in Nyack, New York. They took a much broader, long-range view.

As early as 1981 Mom and Dad agreed to allow a crew from a Boston television station to shoot a local feature about me and the progress I'd made since the accident. A few months later my case was one of several documented by an NBC affiliate in a feature dealing with facial disfigurement. That piece, narrated by a young NBC reporter out of Chicago by the name of Carol Marin, got picked up by the network. Other television appearances followed—including a piece on the *ABC Evening News*.

During this time my mother also signed a contract to write a book about me. Her primary motivation for writing a book was the same as that involved in welcoming the television coverage of my story. As she told my nurse, Betty Dew, "I want to make Joel famous. Then, just maybe, people will accept my son and the way he looks."

My mom made me feel like something special, even before the book came out. I could see it in her eyes whenever she looked at me. I never had any doubt that she loved me just the way I was.

But I did feel like something of a celebrity when Mom's book, *Race for Life*, was published. I remember stacks of books, taller than I was, covering our dining room table, waiting for my autograph. I was certainly tired of printing J-O-E-L long before the promotional hoopla died down. I must have signed a hundred or more some days.

I don't know how famous I became as a result. And it would take years to judge how effective Mom's strategy for gaining acceptance for me would be. But one immediate result of all the media attention I received as a preschooler was that reporters and television cameras became almost as common a part of life as surgery or those daily dressing changes.

And a whole lot less unpleasant.

Chapter 8

When I made my first network television appearance on the *Today* show, I was five—too young to know it was supposed to be a big deal. I wasn't on live with Bryant Gumbel, but my story was told and video of me was shown from the NBC documentary *For Beauty Passed Away* by Carol Marin. She had come to Boston some months earlier to film one of my visits to Shriners Burn Institute. I remember that she asked me and my parents lots of questions. But by the time the program aired on television, I'd almost forgotten about the whole thing. My family and a lot of our friends watched and talked about the program, but I didn't know what the fuss was all about.

My mom and dad went on a lot of television shows to talk about Mom's book when it first came out. Sometimes I went with them. But usually I would stand behind a curtain alongside the set until they were almost done talking. Then some adult who worked at the TV station would tell me, "Now it's time for you to go out there, Joel. Walk around that camera. Watch the cords so you don't trip. Climb that big step onto the set and walk right over and get on your mother's lap. Okay?"

Sometimes I'd have to say a few words. But most of the time I just sat there and waved as the audience applauded. So TV shows never seemed like a big deal to me.

Television reporters, like doctors, talked a lot and asked a bunch of questions. But when we finished talking, the reporters never did anything that hurt me—which was more than I could say about the doctors who continued to make regular appearances in my life.

For me 1983 was a milestone year medically. I had more reconstructive work on my nose. But the big deal was my head. First I had another serious infection in my skull wound that required ten days of treatment in the hospital. A month later, after the infection had cleared up, the doctors brought me back to the hospital, where they scrubbed off the dead portion of my skull bone—until they got down to fresh, healthy bone. Then they watched for a few weeks as fresh, granulated scar tissue began to grow over the bone's surface. When I finally had enough new scar tissue to form a base, they grafted on a flap of skin from my abdomen to completely cover the head wound that had been exposed for almost four years.

The graft took a while to completely heal. But when it finally did, what a change it made in my life! No more agonizing daily dressing changes. No more antiseptic in my eyes. I still wore my helmet for protection everywhere I went. But life was simpler, happier, and better. For me, and for my parents.

From the time of the accident my parents viewed the fall of 1983 as a critical deadline, because that was when I was scheduled to begin public school kindergarten. So in addition to my physical rehabilitation, my folks did everything they could to keep me from falling behind my peers academically.

Perhaps being a scientist made it easier for my dad to anticipate the important role computers would soon play in our world. He saw them as the wave of the future. And since he still didn't know how far physical rehabilitation could take me in the future, he wanted to give me every edge possible by developing my computer skills. Even as a preschooler I had an Apple computer I could play with. Between that and the ColecoVision video game system our friends at the Rockland Volunteer Fire Department had given me, I quickly developed more computer savvy than most of my friends. My favorite game was Pac-Man, and it wasn't long before I could beat my dad and anyone else I could entice into playing it with me.

Preschool not only reinforced the basic knowledge my parents instilled at home (colors, letters of the alphabet, and so on), it had provided me with a small, close-knit peer group in which to practice important socialization skills. So I really was ready for kindergarten. And I don't think I or my parents had any doubts about that. We talked so much about it that I could hardly wait for school to begin that fall.

Of course, my parents had concerns they didn't talk about with me. They had done everything they could to prepare me for school. Now they were wondering, *What more can we do to help prepare the school for Joel?*

When they first went in and spoke to the principal, he was less than enthusiastic about me attending his school. I guess he wasn't sure how much special consideration I would need from his staff. But before long he became one of my biggest advocates and worked tirelessly to make sure the school met my needs.

But when the parents of my preschool classmates heard about the initial reluctance, they went to a meeting at the elementary school to assure the staff and other parents that my presence at Upper Nyack Elementary would not present a hardship to anyone else. The father of one of the little girls in my preschool class, a scientist who regularly flew all over the globe to inspect and certify the safety of the biggest hydroelectric dams in the world, stood up at that meeting and admitted, "When my daughter first wanted to invite Joel over to our house to play, I didn't want him to come. I didn't see why she needed someone like Joel for a friend. But watching their relationship develop, getting to know Joel, has taught me and my family so much. You can be sure that Joel Sonnenberg will be an asset to this school and its students—not a problem for you to worry about."

The authorities were convinced. My parents and the principal talked to the kindergarten teachers. They also conferred with a caseworker from Shriners Children's Hospital in Boston about any other helpful steps that might pave the way for a smooth start to my academic career. And everyone agreed on a plan.

Which is why I played hooky from Upper Nyack Elementary on the very first day of school. A team of professionals (a social worker, two nurses, and the hospital schoolteacher) from Shriners went in my place. They showed a video about me in an assembly program for the whole school. They told the other kids about the accident and answered any questions my future classmates had about my burns and physical limitations. Then this team of professionals traveled from classroom to classroom, allowing the children to express any anxieties and stressing how each child needed to act positively toward me and how they shouldn't act. But mostly they tried to emphasize how, though I looked different, I had the same thoughts and feelings everyone else did. And what's more, because of everything I'd gone through, I'd proved I was a very brave and special boy.

This was the same message my parents had tried to get across for years. It was the biggest motivation for Mom's book. She talked about it in the book and in interviews with newspaper reporters, saying, "We feel an urgent need to communicate with the world about our son. We want him to be treated with respect and dignity. We don't want him to be rejected, to be looked upon with horror, fear, or disgust. We don't want the world to be a fearful place for Joel."

The strategy worked. When I walked through the front doors of Upper Nyack Elementary for the first time on the morning of the second day of school, everyone wanted to be my friend.

Most of my preschool pals went to kindergarten at Upper Nyack. So that also helped make my adjustment to public school an easy and positive one. I wanted nothing more than to fit in and do everything my classmates were doing. My teacher and the school staff seemed to understand that, and they worked with me toward that goal.

At the same time that I was working to fit into the general school population as much as possible, I experienced a growing awareness of the differences between me and my classmates. I don't think this had as much to do with the new public school setting as it did the fact that I was growing up—gaining both maturity and a greater sense of self-awareness in the process.

"We want him to be treated with respect and dignity. We don't want the world to be a fearful place for Joel."

One obvious difference was that nobody I knew went to the hospital as often as I did. Some friend might get tubes put in his ears or have his tonsils taken out. But for other people, those were once-in-a-lifetime deals, whereas hospitalizations continued to be a frequent part of my routine. Not just unpleasant, often painful experiences, but constant interruptions of my life that made me feel different from other people.

In the beginning, right after the accident, all the operations had been done just to ensure my survival—covering burn sites, trying to prevent infection and additional tissue loss. Once the doctors became convinced I would live, many of the subsequent surgeries were designed to improve my quality of life—widening my mouth so I could eat, shaping the end of my left arm to better fit a prosthesis, constructing a right hand so I could manipulate objects and be able to better care for myself.

But by the time I started school, I'd reached a point in my recovery where more of the medical decisions yet to be made seemed to involve cosmetic considerations. While my medical team just naturally seemed to feel they needed to do everything possible to improve my appearance, fortunately my parents realized the toll those operations were taking on me. So even at the tender age of five or six, whenever the possibility of another medical procedure came up, Mom and Dad began including me in the discussion and the decision-making process.

After more than thirty surgical procedures, part of me was ready to declare, "Enough already! No more operations!" But it wasn't quite that simple.

"The doctors are talking about another operation on your nose, Joel."

"Why?"

"They say it will make your nose look more like other people's noses."

"I don't care about that."

"They also say it will help you breathe a lot better when you run hard and play soccer."

"Okay then."

Or . . .

"When you were little the doctors operated to give you a larger mouth opening and keep the food from dribbling down your chin. Now the doctor says he can take some of the pink tissue from inside your mouth and make you a nice new set of lips."

"Why do I need lips? I don't want the operation."

More work on reconstructing eyelids made sense to me. My eyes needed protection and had a tendency to dry out without drops. Working eyelids would help keep my eyes lubricated. It would require a series of surgeries, first on one side and then the other.

What about earlobes? Mine had burned off. Yet I could hear well enough through the remaining ear holes on the side of my head. I decided I didn't need earlobes.

Very quickly my primary consideration with medical decisions involved function rather than appearance. If I was convinced an operation would improve my health or somehow make my life measurably better, I was willing to endure another procedure. But if all the doctors could offer were cosmetic "advantages," I told my parents I wasn't interested. And they honored my wishes. Never did I have any procedure done simply for the sake of appearance.

But avoiding the pain and hassle of surgery wasn't the only factor in my decision making. I felt the same way looking in the mirror and imagining the results of cosmetic surgery plans as I felt about the prosthesis with the hook. That's just not me.

I had the same reaction, maybe even stronger, when I was given the option of wearing a wig to cover my burned bald head. One of the counselors at the hospital had a teenage patient come into the room and model a hairpiece for me. It looked fine on him. But I couldn't help remembering a visit to Michigan when my sisters, some of my cousins, and I found one of my grandma's wigs in her bedroom and took turns trying it on. We all looked different (and pretty funny) with gray hair. But I looked the most different and drew the most laughs of all.

So whenever the idea of wearing a wig came up, I tried to imagine how it would look on me. Then I immediately decided, *That's really not me*.

My lack of interest in cosmetic changes doesn't mean I was particularly thrilled with my appearance. But I didn't have to be. I'd grown accustomed to the way I looked. That was me! In fact, I thought I looked a lot like ET in one of my all-time favorite movies. Everyone loved ET. Nobody thought he needed plastic surgery. Besides, I had finally gained what felt like a small measure of control over my own life by having a say as to whether any more operations seemed worth it.

Still, there continued to be some surgeries we all agreed were necessary. And while you might think all my past experiences would make those easier to face, you'd be wrong. The truth was, past experience often added to my dread. I knew very well what was coming.

That was certainly true on one memorable trip back to Boston. I don't even remember which procedure was scheduled. I just know I didn't want to go through another hospital stay, another operation, and another recovery. But there I was, sitting all by myself in the back of the family station wagon. Mom sat behind the wheel, rolling along the Massachusetts Turnpike toward Boston, when I announced, "I don't want another operation."

Mom glanced up in the rearview mirror. "I know, Joel. It's hard to keep going through these operations. But you can know that God will always be with you."

I don't remember what triggered my next question. Maybe a previous discussion with my parents, or perhaps a recent Sunday school lesson. But when she mentioned God always being with me, I asked, "Mom, how do you know you're going to heaven to be with God when you die?"

Mom sensed this was a serious question. "If you believe in Jesus," my mother replied thoughtfully, "and ask him into your heart, then the Bible says you will go to heaven when you die. Of course, we never know when that might be. Some people get sick and die. Or they are killed in an accident. Or during surgery. Or we may just get so old and weak that we die. We never know when our time will come. But if we know Jesus, we don't have to worry about dying because we know, whenever it happens, we're going to heaven to be with him." Mom paused. "Joel, do you believe in Jesus?"

"Yes," I assured her.

"Did you ever ask him to come into your heart and be your Savior, so that no matter what happens, you'll know you are going to be in heaven with him?"

"No." I didn't remember ever doing that.

"Would you like to do that right now?" she asked.

"Yes, Mama."

So my mother began to pray with me as we drove down the highway. "Thank you, Lord, that you saved Joel's life for a purpose. He's worried about another surgery right now. He really doesn't want to go through this again. And I don't blame him. But we know you will be with him. And right now Joel wants to make sure you will be with him forever."

Mom told me I needed to pray myself. And she led me in what to say: "Jesus, please come into my heart and be my Savior. Forgive me for the wrong things I have done. And help me follow you the rest of my life. Amen."

I knew that Jesus comforted me when I was hurting and life seemed out of my control.

Some people may think I wasn't old enough to make a meaningful spiritual decision at that age. But I did. I understood that Jesus and I were going to be together forever. And while I can't say it was the end of all my anxiety over surgeries, I can say that, from then on, whenever my parents had to leave me in the hospital overnight, I always knew for a fact that I was never alone. I knew that Jesus comforted me when I was hurting and life seemed out of my control, and that he knew what I was going through, even when no one else did.

One of the most painful parts of any surgical experience for me, and perhaps the most dreaded, came before every operation. I was so badly scarred that it was virtually impossible for anyone to find a place to insert an intravenous line in my arms or legs. I'd had a couple of nurses actually faint as they watched a doctor probe futilely around my head and neck, looking for a likely spot. The only easy access to a good working vein was in my groin.

So for years, before every surgery, the very last thing I remember in the operating room was an embarrassing sense of exposure, followed by the painful probing for a vein, then the agony of a plastic tube being forced into one of the most sensitive areas of my body. Minutes later, after they started dripping anesthesia into that tube, I would finally drift off to sleep.

On one of my hospital visits at about this age I complained about this to my mother, who was sitting near the bed in my room, waiting for an orderly to come and wheel me to the OR. Her response was, "Maybe they could give you gas so you could be asleep before they put the IV in."

That sounded great to me.

A nurse who happened to walk into the room right around that time told us, "I don't see why we can't do that. It won't hurt to ask."

So Mom asked an OR nurse. Her response was, "Sure! We can do that." Like it was no big deal at all.

But it was a huge deal for me. From then on, bubblegum- or watermelon-scented gas (my favorite choices) enabled me to sleep blissfully through what had always seemed to be the worst part of any surgery for me. And the fact that medical people had listened restored for me another small sense of control over my own medical care.

Of course, there continued to be too many things over which I still had little or no control. Like the surgery I had on my right hand the spring of my kindergarten year.

As far as I was concerned, the hand that the doctors had created for me worked very well. My "pincher," as I called it, enabled me to pick up and manipulate everything from clothes to silverware to pencils to computer-game joysticks to toy soldiers. Without it I would have been almost totally dependent.

But my reconstructed hand wasn't going to grow in proportion with my body. The doctors convinced all of us that, if I was going to get maximum lifelong use out of my hand as I got bigger, it needed to be longer. And in order for that to happen, it would require a contraption the doctors called a "distraction device."

I should have known any procedure that began with the doctors fracturing every bone in my hand wasn't going to be much fun. And it wasn't.

During the initial operation in which they broke the bones, they also inserted pins in those bones, ran a wire through the pins, and placed the whole hand in a wire cage that would enclose and protect the hand for several months. Each day my parents would turn a key attached to the wire, pulling the sections of the bone a little farther apart. The idea was to stimulate ossification by forcing the body to fill in the gaps and thus make the bones that much longer and my hand larger.

For a while everything seemed to be proceeding as planned. After I recovered from the initial surgery, the wire cage around my hand proved more of an annoyance than a pain. Once again I had to depend on other people to feed me. And it severely limited my play. I couldn't even go swimming for fear of infection getting in around the pins. The prospects for a fun and exciting summer didn't look good.

However, late that spring, my parents received a surprise phone call from old family friends who said they'd been praying about what to do with some unexpected money and felt the Lord was telling them to give it to the Sonnenbergs for a much-needed family vacation. About the same time a college buddy of Dad's invited us to spend some time on his working ranch out in Colorado. So the whole family packed up (with so many medical supplies there was hardly enough room for clothes in our suitcases) and headed west.

We saw mountains and wild animals. We met real cowboys. We rode horses. It was a once-in-a-lifetime, dream-come-true adventure for any six-year-old boy—if I hadn't had my one and only hand confined in an unwieldy cage and wrapped and padded for additional "protection."

I did enjoy the horseback riding. But I felt like a spectator watching my sisters doing fun stuff I couldn't or wasn't allowed to do. They climbed fences, fed and played with farm animals, went swimming, fished, and ran all over the ranch.

In addition to the frustration of feeling limited, I was also hurting. As time had gone on, the daily tightening of the distraction device had begun to feel different. The pain got so bad I felt certain it was doing more harm than good. I begged my parents to stop. I hoped they'd get so busy enjoying the vacation they'd forget to turn the key some days. I certainly wouldn't bother to remind them.

One day, near the end of our time in Colorado, Dad was giving the key its usual daily turn. I felt the pressure building and again tried to tell him to stop, but it was too late. When we heard the audible "crack" in my hand, we both knew something inside had broken. If that sound wasn't enough to convince Dad, my immediate reaction was.

My screaming cut short yet another family vacation.

Everyone came running.

When they couldn't get me calmed down, Mom and Dad decided I needed to see a doctor. But there we were in southern Colorado—miles from any town. It would take the better part of a day to drive to any major hospital.

So our friends called a neighboring rancher who owned a small plane and explained the emergency. He immediately agreed to fly the whole family to Denver.

That, too, might have been a wonderfully memorable experience, soaring like an eagle just above the tops of some of the highest peaks in the Rocky Mountains—if I'd have been in any shape to enjoy it.

I think I screamed the entire way. And when a fierce afternoon storm blew in from the west, I couldn't decide which was the more miserable sensation—the unbearable pain in my hand, or the sick churning of my stomach as the winds buffeted that plane up and down like the most terrifying roller-coaster ride ever devised.

When we finally landed safely in Denver, the entire Sonnenberg clan breathed a huge sigh of relief and vowed never to go up in a small plane again. The doctors in Denver relieved the pressure on the wire, confirmed that a bone had been broken, prescribed a painkiller, and recommended we go back to Boston for follow-up as soon as possible.

So we didn't even get a chance to rest up from our "vacation" before we were off on another trip to Shriners, where the doctors decided the broken bones in my hand were healing and were already definitely longer. The distraction device had done its job.

What a relief to have that thing off so I could go about my regular routines at church and at school—starting first grade, playing soccer. The only operation I had all year required a four-day hospital stay for doctors to reconstruct my upper right and lower left eyelids. And we even managed a very special vacation trip that spring—one that didn't end in a medical emergency.

In March of my first-grade year, the Shriners asked me to be one of the guest speakers for their annual $100 million dollar fund-raising dinner in Orlando, Florida. They flew the whole family down for the occasion. One of our hosts met us at the plane and gave us a limo ride to our hotel—complete with police escort through all the red lights. Then I got to pick from a dozen dune buggies the one I'd ride in for a parade that would take us on a personal tour of Orlando.

The night of the dinner the hotel ballroom was packed with people who paid $1000 a plate. I was too young to make a real speech, but the emcee called me up on the platform, told the audience about my accident, and listed the different procedures done for me at Shriners Hospital in Boston. He also read special letters of commendation sent to me by Florida governor Bob Graham and by the president of the United States, Ronald Reagan. When the emcee was done, my dad lifted me up on his shoulders so everyone could see me as I called out, "Thank you for your hospitals!"

The entire ballroom erupted as everyone stood to cheer and applaud.

But the real highlight of the Orlando trip for me was the day our whole family went to Disney World. The Shriners arranged for celebrity treatment. Not only were we ushered to the front of every line, but I also personally met and had my picture taken with every major Disney character from Snow White to Mickey himself. What more could any kid ask for?

Chapter 9

I think it was experiences like our Colorado vacation and our special Disney World trip that fueled my parents' determination to help me experience as normal a childhood as possible. But "normal" wasn't always easy for me.

Riding a bike proved a challenge at first. So much did I identify with Hollywood's favorite extraterrestrial, that I'd asked for and gotten an "ET bike," just like the one in the movie. I used training wheels for a while, but when we'd take them off, I'd tip right over. Dad would run along behind, holding the bike up, but the moment he'd let go I would lose my balance. I have no idea how much of the problem was the usual learning curve all kids go through, or whether it was that much harder for me to control my balance and the bike without hands to grip the handlebars.

Dad and I both probably wondered if I'd ever ride a bike. And after a couple of unsuccessful practice sessions on my two-wheeler, I tried to be content with riding my Big Wheel tricycle up and down the sidewalk and around the yard.

Then one day I went with a bunch of my buddies to the house of a friend who lived at the bottom of a hill at the end of a quiet cul-de-sac. Naturally, all the guys pushed their bikes to the top of the hill and came racing down. I couldn't go quite as fast on my Big Wheel, but I made a lot more noise, which appealed to one of my friends. So he asked to trade with me for a couple of turns.

I wasn't about to admit to all my friends that I still couldn't ride a two-wheeler, so I told him, "Sure!" Then I pushed his bike up the incline, trying to figure out, *How am I going to do this?* By the time I got to the top of the hill, I'd thought up what seemed like a workable strategy.

Pointing the bike down the hill, I climbed on. Thankfully, the bike was small enough that my feet touched the ground if I really stretched. So I started to slowly coast down the slope, with both feet dragging to provide me just enough stability to stay upright. I made it all the way to the bottom and decided to try again. A little faster this time—dragging my feet a little less. The third time I got up enough speed that when I reached the bottom of the hill I just lifted my feet and coasted to a stop. The time after that, when I got to the bottom, I lifted my feet, and instead of coasting, I decided to start pedaling. Wow! Just like that, I was riding a bike.

I don't remember how long it was after that before the whole family took me to a parking lot on the Nyack College campus so Dad could give me another bike-riding lesson. I climbed on, and Dad offered a few last-minute instructions and began to push. I started pedaling, and Dad was really chugging to keep up and hang on. When he finally ran out of gas and let go, I kept right on going.

For a few seconds I think my parents were too surprised to react. Then they began to cheer and applaud. "Look at you! All right, Joel. Way to go!" I grinned with pride.

Mom cried. Which I really didn't understand at the time.

I didn't know she was recalling all those days she'd sat by my bed in the hospital in the first weeks after the accident, watching me lose my fingers and toes and then my hands. When the doctors had said I'd never be able to walk, she'd tried to imagine what my future would be like. Never being able to run. Never riding a bike. Never being able to do so many things . . .

Watching me take off on the bike that day brought back all those memories. Joel can ride a bike! My future wasn't nearly as limited as she'd feared. Mom was so happy she cried.

First graders don't think a lot about their future. Fortunately, my parents did. Even during those early days after the accident, when most of the family's concern and energy had to be focused on day-to-day survival, my parents—especially my dad—thought a lot about my future. And now that some of the daily demands had eased up and the biggest medical issues had been successfully dealt with, they began discussing how best to prepare me for that future.

The Nyack community—both the college and the town—had been very supportive of our family. But the older I got and the more aware and sensitive I was becoming to people's reactions, the more my folks began to think I might do better in a different setting. Nyack only looked like a small and sheltered village on the west bank of the Hudson River. It was actually very much a part of metropolitan New York.

While I didn't have to face Disney-size crowds every day, there were countless strangers wherever we went—whether we took in a movie as a family, shopped at the mall, or ate at a nearby restaurant. So there were always lots of stares.

My response varied according to my mood. Usually I tried to ignore the stares—to at least act as if I didn't notice people's reactions to me. But more and more I *did* notice. And sometimes I couldn't help responding.

One of my favorite responses was to stare back. That often embarrassed people into looking away. And I occasionally still did what my mother had suggested for years. I'd smile right at the person and say, "My name is Joel. What's yours?" If I felt someone was being particularly obnoxious or rude, I might ask, "What are you looking at?" I found if I got them to speak to me, they almost always quit staring. Once in a while we'd actually have a nice conversation.

But there were occasional encounters with strangers when there just wasn't much to say. Some people would get up and leave a restaurant when our family walked in. I vividly recall one waitress who walked up to our table, spotted me, gasped, and muttered, "That's disgusting." My mother had a few things to say to her.

I doubt those sorts of encounters occurred any more often than they had when I was younger; I probably was just more aware of them—and definitely more sensitive to what other people thought about me. So it's not surprising that my parents began to wonder if there would be less of that sort of unpleasantness in a smaller community where more people knew me and would be familiar enough with me and my story that they wouldn't be shocked or feel the need to stare.

Any thoughts of moving to another part of the country meant rethinking the source of my medical care. As grateful as my folks were to the Shriners Hospital in Boston for all the free treatment they'd provided me (maybe fortysome operations by this time), they were ready to move on if need be.

Since they were considering a move back to the Midwest, my parents took me to the renowned burn center at the University of Michigan for an assessment. When the experts there said that their U of M research had found that young burn survivors who made the best adjustment were those who lived and grew up in small rural communities, it confirmed what my parents had already suspected. And it helped clinch their decision: the Sonnenbergs were moving to Michigan, where we would be a lot closer to relatives and a family support system.

The summer after my first-grade year we loaded up all our belongings and left the only home I'd ever known to move to Canton, Michigan—a town near relatives, not far from Detroit. The transition was a lot tougher on my parents and my older sister, Jami, than it was on me. Any sadness I felt in saying good-bye to my friends was tempered by the fact that I was too young to realize that moving halfway across the country meant I might never see them again. As long as my family would be there, I wasn't worried about anything. We'd be a lot closer to grandparents and cousins. And what sounded best of all was that the house we were moving into had a swimming pool in the backyard. Once I heard that, I could hardly wait.

I didn't know that the primary reason for a swimming pool was to provide me with physical therapy. Nor did I know that even before they signed the rental agreement, my parents had checked out the local school district. They asked the special services coordinator of the school system in Nyack to talk to his counterpart in Canton. Then Mom talked to Joyce Darren, the principal of the school I would attend, to talk about me and my needs. Mrs. Darren not only assured Mom I would be welcome in her school; she said, "I know a number of the families in your subdivision. I'll be glad to call and talk to them to pave the way for you and Joel in the neighborhood." Which helps explain what happened on the day we moved in . . .

The last of the furniture was barely off the moving truck when I shouted, "Let's go swimming everybody!" Before my parents could stop us, Jami, Sommer, and I had dashed out the door and headed to the pool. By the time Mom got outside, I'd stripped to my shorts and was already testing the amount of spring in the diving board.

I saw no reason for the concern in my mother's eyes. I had no idea she was silently wondering, *Dear God, what's going to happen now?* In her mind all the hours, days, and months of planning my transition into our new community were about to be put to the test with a simple swim. What were the neighbor kids going to say and do when they saw me standing on the diving board with all my scars uncovered and in full view? In their worst fears, my parents envisioned a lineup of rude kids standing at our fence and pointing, gasping, and heckling, *Look at him!*

But that wasn't what happened at all.

Within minutes a tall, dark-haired boy showed up at our fence. "Hi, Joel!" he cheerfully announced. "My name is John." After he ran off, two others took his place—a medium-sized, brown-haired boy, "Joel, my name is Curt." "Hi, Joel, my name is Alan." Before long there were at least ten kids—all different ages, boys and girls—waving and welcoming me with their smiles of excitement.

Even though I was only six years old at the time, I remember that scene to this day. Our neighbors didn't just make us feel welcome; they treated me like a celebrity who had moved in next door. My mother couldn't quit smiling. All the hours of preparation my parents and others had made was paying off in those first few minutes outside our fence on that sunny Michigan afternoon.

By the second day, and for the rest of that summer, most of those kids were inside our fence, playing and swimming with me in our pool. Making me feel very much at home in our new Michigan neighborhood, even before the memories of my old friends in Nyack had begun to fade away.

When fall rolled around, the administration and staff at Gallimore Elementary School saw to it that my transition to my new school went just as smoothly. Once again I skipped the first day of classes. The principal showed videos of me, including clips from a television documentary, to all the students in the school. When the students asked questions, she answered as honestly as she could, emphasizing, as always, the fact that the burns on the outside of my body didn't change who I was on the inside. That I was a seven-year-old boy who had all the same feelings they did. And, of course, that I was especially brave.

By the time I walked into Gallimore Elementary School, anyone who hadn't already met me around our backyard pool wanted to. Up and down the halls people waved, smiled, and said, "Hi, Joel!"

On the one hand, all the friendly attention was nice. Yet I found it a little disconcerting. "Everyone at school knows my name," I complained to my parents, "but I don't know theirs!"

A week or so after school began there was a Parent-Teacher Association (PTA) meeting and an open house at Gallimore Elementary. I remember walking down the hall, holding my mother's hand as first a teacher, then an older student, and after that the parent of a student I didn't even recognize each greeted me warmly:

"Glad you could come, Joel."

"Hey, Joel."

"Hello, Joel."

"See what I mean?" I complained to my mom. "They all know me."

I didn't understand then why my mother was grinning at my aggravation.

Second grade proved to be a great time for me. I only went to the hospital once during that whole school year—so the plastic surgeons could do a little more work on my left upper eyelid. Plus, I suffered a cellulitis infection in my right leg. That was it. The rest of the year I was free to concentrate on school and just being a kid.

I loved my teacher—Mrs. Foster. She bragged on my penmanship. (I did have some of the neatest printing in my class.) I also made great strides in developing my reading skills and even "wrote and published" two books of my own as class projects. Outside of school I continued to play soccer and became even more of a local celebrity when TV reporter Carol Marin showed up in Canton with a camera crew to update my story for another NBC documentary special—*For Beauty Passed Away (Continued)*.

As great as the school was, as nice as it felt to be known and accepted around the community, and as wonderful as it was not to be in and out of the hospital so many times, there was something else that made this year memorable and special for me. It was the sense of independence and freedom I felt living in what was still pretty much a semirural community. I wasn't old enough to understand why the experts had recommended it to my parents. But I certainly would have recommended it to anyone.

The timing couldn't have been better for me. Everything seemed to come together. Most of the medical concerns eased up at the very same time I'd reached an age when my parents could trust me with some personal independence. All at the very same time we moved to a place where a boy could roam and explore to his heart's content.

Unlike Nyack, New York, all the streets were flat and great for bike riding. And we lived at the end of a quiet cul-de-sac, so we could play safely out in the street, which I thought was pretty neat.

While we lived in a fairly typical suburban-looking neighborhood, our home was located near the edge of a subdivision bordered by farmlands and forests that soon became my personal playground. I rode my bike over trails through the woods in the summer and fall. I fished, hunted snails and crawdads and salamanders, and waded in the nearby stream in all sorts of weather. In the winter I donned heavy boots to trek through snowy fields and slip-slide over the surface of the frozen creek. I chased rabbits and deer just to see them run. I watched birds build nests and feed their young. This boy who'd spent much of his childhood confined to a hospital room discovered a sense of freedom I'd never known before. I found that God's great outdoors held an attraction for me that not even Walt Disney could match.

The minnows I caught in the creek came home and actually lived in an aquarium in my bedroom. Until one day they all jumped out while we were gone, and we returned home to the smell of the dead fish that were scattered all over my floor.

That whole second-grade year was such a wonderful time of discovery for me that my parents were forever convinced that the researchers were right—a rural setting was certainly an ideal place for their burn-survivor son to grow up. Unfortunately, the harsh Midwestern weather—both the winter cold and summer humidity—presented added hardship for someone with my injuries.

So my parents began discussing another move. And after extensive searching, Dad pinpointed two places in the country that offered what our family needed in a rural setting with moderate climate. One of those places was Montreat, North Carolina, just outside of Asheville, where there just happened to be a small Christian college that needed a biology professor with Dad's experience and credentials.

In some ways I had a tougher time leaving Michigan after one year than I'd had moving from our longtime home in Nyack the year before. I guess I better understood what it meant to move and leave friends and relatives behind. Leaving my swimming pool was part of it. Nor did I want to leave the familiar trails through what I'd come to think of as my woods, my fields, and my creek.

What I had no way of realizing at the time was what a great year of transition Michigan had been for all of us. And what a wonderful preparation it had been for the greater adventures that lay ahead in the even more rural mountains of North Carolina.

Chapter 10

The first adventure was the trip I took with Dad, just the two of us, to deliver the initial U-Haul load of our family possessions to the house in Montreat where we were going to live. I still remember the spectacular view coming over the Smoky Mountains at about dusk. The mountaintops caught the last golden rays of the day's sunshine as we wound down through dark-green shadowed valleys toward our new home.

Montreat itself is a tiny hamlet of four hundred or so people, tucked way back up in a deep, narrow valley fifteen miles east of Asheville. It isn't big enough to have its own downtown. The nearest store is three miles down the road in Black Mountain.

The heart of Montreat was the four hundred-student Christian liberal arts college by the same name (where Dad was going to teach) and a Presbyterian assembly grounds that hosted thousands of conferees and visitors every year. The one road into Montreat winds along Flat Creek (which is anything but flat) at the very bottom of the valley. A handful of very narrow intersecting streets wind up the steep mountain slopes on one side of the creek or the other. But the only way out of town is back down through Black Mountain on the same road you came in on—unless you want to test your four-wheel drive on some rugged U.S. Forest Service trail heading up into the mountain wilderness toward Mount Mitchell, the highest peak in the eastern United States.

Many of Montreat's residents were somehow affiliated with the college or the conference center. Retired Presbyterian ministers or missionaries made up a good percentage of the population. Billy Graham and his wife, Ruth, lived in a log house at the end of a steep, winding driveway just up the mountain above our home. A number of staff people with the Billy Graham Evangelistic Association also lived nearby.

After spending a year living in a typical modern subdivision planted among flat Midwestern cornfields, I could not believe how different this felt. We still had neighbors, but their houses weren't alongside ours. They were hidden in the trees high above, or they were far below us on the mountainside. It made us feel as though we were surrounded by nothing but wooded mountain wilderness, which I was eager to explore. And when people told us that black bears wandered down into town every winter looking for food, I could hardly wait for the weather to turn cold.

In the meantime, I made a little excitement of my own soon after moving in, with the help of some older boys who lived nearby. Unfortunately, those adventures weren't the best introduction I could have had to the town of Montreat.

As an eight-year-old I was naturally more of a follower than a leader—especially in a new setting with neighborhood guys I wanted very much to impress. But as much as I'd like to, I can't blame my new friends. I was old enough to know better.

In fact, the first incident began with me questioning a friend I'll call Joe as I followed him through the woods toward a house left empty when a family moved out of the neighborhood. "Where are we going?" I wanted to know.

"Just come on," he told me. So I did.

I should have turned back the second I heard glass breaking. "What are you doing?" I asked before I saw him smash the second window.

"You comin' or not?" Joe demanded as he reached through the broken window and opened the back door.

What the heck? I knew there was no one home. I didn't want to seem like a big chicken. And there was something of a thrill in walking into a deserted house.

Every footstep and every whisper seemed to echo as we walked from room to empty room. The only things left in the entire place were window shades, carpeting, and a thin layer of dust that had accumulated since the last family moved out—until we got to the kitchen, and there on the counter was a large container of wood glue. "Hey, watch this!" my buddy said as he popped open the top and began drizzling the glue all over the floor.

By the time we slipped out of the house a few minutes later I was wishing I was somewhere else. Anywhere else. I split from my friend as soon as I could, but by the time I got home I was already feeling guilty.

I tried my best to put the whole incident out of my mind. But a few days later I overheard my parents discussing the vandalism that had the whole neighborhood talking. When the new family that was planning to move in discovered the broken windows and the glue, they didn't know what to think. They didn't know whether or not to take it personally—did someone not want them moving into the house? They even worried that the neighborhood wasn't safe.

I had never thought that what we did might scare someone, and it made me feel even more guilty. In fact, I got to feeling so convicted that I finally told my parents what had happened.

I think they were as surprised as they were upset. And no doubt embarrassed. They went to the people who were buying the house to explain what had happened and to assure them I'd never done anything like this before. I had to apologize and agree to do chores for my parents to pay for the windows. We all went over and worked forever to clean up the hardened glue. By the time we finished I had determined never to try that stunt again.

Before I knew it, summer was almost over and it was time for a new school year to start. Mom took me to visit Black Mountain Primary School ahead of time so I could meet my principal, Mr. Green, and my third-grade teacher, Mrs. Bartlett. They acted pleased that I was going to be in their school. But once again I missed the first day of classes as my parents went in my stead and took a video of me to show to all the other students. So for the third time in my short academic career I walked into a new school where everyone knew my name and almost everyone wanted to be my friend.

Unfortunately, I was still seeking friendship and acceptance from some of the older boys who lived near me in Montreat. Which is why I got in trouble again early that fall.

It happened one afternoon when a bunch of us piled off the school bus down at the end of our street and began the steep uphill hike home. As we walked past the lot where a new house was going in, we noticed that the construction crew had already knocked off for the day. So one of the other guys picked up a small stone and threw it at the house, where it pinged off a window without doing any damage. I laughed rather scornfully and asked, "Can't you throw any harder than that?" Then I picked up a larger rock and let it fly.

Crrash! I shattered the window on my very first try. I got this sick feeling in the pit of my stomach. But my buddy seemed impressed. He picked up a bunch of stones and began hurling them at the front of the house. One of them finally found the mark, and the second loud crash brought a neighbor man rushing down his driveway and shouting, "What's going on down there?"

When the cluster of kids immediately scattered in every direction, I instinctively turned and started to run as well. But I'd only taken a couple of steps when the thought hit me: *Who am I trying to fool? There's no way he's not going to recognize me. How many other one-handed kids are going to be running around our Montreat neighborhood?*

I stopped and faced the music. It wasn't pleasant. My parents seemed much more upset at this second incident of vandalism than they had been at the first. They not only saw the makings of a pattern; they also had to be concerned about my reputation in the community.

I wondered what price I was going to have to pay this time. But instead of telling me what was going to happen, I remember Dad asking me, "What do you think your punishment ought to be, Joel?"

Oh, man! If I made a suggestion he thought was too light, he might just decide to punish me big-time. At the same time I didn't want to be unnecessarily hard on myself. So I didn't know what to say.

"Think about it, Joel."

I didn't want to think about it. I wanted to get the whole thing over with! I told my father I would earn the money to pay for replacing the windows. (I was quickly learning that the price of vandalism was a lot higher than any thrill was worth.) And, of course, I was grounded—for how long or from what I don't recall. What I do remember, and it made me feel far worse than any punishment, was my parents' disappointment.

All my life they had told me how proud they were of me. They said it not just with words but with their eyes and in the way they introduced me to their friends and the way they reacted when strangers stared or made rude comments about me. So to realize I'd embarrassed my parents again, to see that disappointment in their eyes, hurt far more than any punishment they might have dreamed up.

Not only did I tell myself I was never going to get into that kind of trouble again, but I decided I needed a different group of friends. A better group of guys to hang around with.

That's when Ryan Councill came into my life. He, too, was in Mrs. Bartlett's third-grade class, a bright, quiet kid who was friendly enough but didn't really stand out or merit any special attention from me the first few weeks of school. The turning point came one day in the school auditorium when we were fatefully united by our adjacent seat placement and by a shared lack of interest in the square dance instruction being offered to our class that day.

I have no idea what prompted him, but right there, sitting in the school auditorium, Ryan told me he had a learning disability. Surprised, I asked him what he meant. He explained that something in the way his brain worked made reading and math especially difficult for him. He had to study harder and longer than other kids just to get by. He talked a little about how it made him feel different from everyone else in class. I could relate to that, so I talked a little about how different I felt. All in all, it was a surprisingly honest conversation between a couple of eight-year-old boys.

We definitely made for an interesting pair, though I don't think I appreciated the irony until many years later. There was Ryan—this handsome (at least all the girls thought so) guy who looked great on the outside but felt unlike other people because his brain didn't always work the way other people's minds did. Here I was—outwardly so different from my classmates in appearance, yet inwardly experiencing the same thoughts and emotions as everyone else. So in a strange sort of way we complemented each other. And though we could never have predicted it at the starting point of our friendship, we would continue to complement each other in many ways for years to come.

While I immediately felt a very special bond with Ryan, my teacher and my classmates also gave me a real sense of acceptance and belonging. In November, for my birthday, I invited everyone in Mrs. Bartlett's room to my party. I think my mom hoped a handful would show up, at least enough to make me feel like we had a real party. When everyone in my class indicated they were coming, I don't know if Mom was more shocked or pleased. She quickly decided we couldn't host the crowd at our house, so she called the college and booked a meeting room big enough to handle everyone who showed up. Which turned out to be quite a crowd.

Such positive experiences did indeed help make me feel accepted by my peers. Not that the acceptance was a surprise. I'd expected a big turnout. At the same time I knew I couldn't ever take the reaction of my classmates for granted.

I had worked hard to fit in, to be like everyone else, and to do what everyone else did. So it was encouraging to see my efforts pay off, because some of those efforts had come at a high price.

I hadn't been at Black Mountain Primary very long when I learned that the school's Parent-Teacher Organization (PTO) regularly sponsored what everyone seemed to think were the biggest social events of the year—roller-skating parties.

Of course, I knew what roller skating was. It looked like fun. I refused to let the fact that I'd never been roller skating deter me. *If this is what everyone in North Carolina did for fun, then I'd just have to learn. How hard can it be?*

Harder than I thought! It's not easy being just like everyone else at a roller-skating party if you've never gone skating before. I might have known this wasn't going to be my favorite sport when I got my pair of skates at the rental counter and had to ask another kid to help me lace them up. So much for wanting to be just like everyone else.

I sat and watched the skaters for a while, trying to learn what I could about proper technique and form. The best skaters glided almost effortlessly around the rink—studies in graceful, smooth, and fluid motion. They made it look so simple.

It wasn't. And only one part of my problem was lack of experience.

I soon learned there was much more to skating than meets the eye. And my own physical limitations proved to be unexpected obstacles.

Due to the extensive scars on my feet and ankles, I can't walk heel-to-toe like most people do. My ankles just don't flex very much. So I walk (and run) on the balls of my feet. It gave me a rather distinctive gait, but it didn't translate all that well to roller skating.

I soon found it was impossible to be smooth and fluid when you skate on the balls of your feet. My style was more herky-jerky. I didn't so much glide as run on my skates. I could get up a pretty impressive head of steam in the length of the rink. Then I would coast. But that presented another problem.

Both stopping and turning required ankle movements I couldn't make. So I crashed into the walls a lot. Several times, to avoid serious collisions with other skaters, I would drop to my knees on the concrete floor. Ouch! But I didn't mind. Pain was the price I paid for many new activities. And sometimes they even required blood.

Every time I went down, someone would rush over and want to know, "Are you okay, Joel?" It was so embarrassing. I figured they probably thought I was a real klutz. The truth was, I very quickly began to get a feel for skating. I knew I could have been one of those smooth, graceful skaters—if only my ankles still worked the way God had designed them to work.

Evidently I should have worried more about my knees than my ankles, because the moment I walked in the door at home, Mom took one look at me and exclaimed, "Oh, Joel! What happened?"

I looked down to see what she was staring at and saw the splotches of blood-stains seeping through my trouser legs. Every time I'd fallen I'd broken through the tight, paper-thin layer of scar tissue that covered my knees. The blood from those wounds now covered both shins and was seeping down into my socks.

Mom helped me wash off the blood and patch up the tears in the skin on my knees. And I laid in bed a long time that night, thinking about the skating party and trying to figure out a better way of stopping myself next time.

I made a lot better impression on people by way of another PTO activity— even though pride wasn't my primary motivation at the time. If I had to admit my true motive, I'd have to call it pure, unadulterated eight-year-old envy.

I remember sitting in the elementary school auditorium and staring up at the stage in awe and wonder. The object of my desire, glistening like a treasure under the spotlights, was a new, shiny, red bicycle.

My first thought was, *Wow! I've gotta have that!*

So when Mr. Green, the principal, told us, "One of you is going to get this bike," my response was, *OH! YESSSS!* I couldn't believe my good fortune, because I knew, "One of you" was gonna be me.

Mr. Green explained that the bike would be awarded to the student who sold the most merchandise in the PTO's annual Christmas fund-raiser. Whoever sold the most wrapping paper and gift items could choose as his or her first-place prize the red bike—or a huge, comparably priced stereo boom box.

As far as I was concerned, there was no comparison. Nor was there any doubt in my mind about who was going to claim first place. That bike was as good as mine!

There remained the small matter of the gift-wrap sales. But my parents had always told me I could do anything I set my mind to. And I believed them. So as far as I was concerned, it was a done deal. I'd take my order book around the neighborhood and start selling that very day.

I like to think of that sales contest as my first real introduction to the people of Montreat. (It was certainly better than the troubling introduction I'd provided myself a few months earlier by breaking windows and vandalizing the neighborhood.)

Selling gift wrap and holiday trinkets seemed pretty easy to me. I didn't have to visit many houses before I refined my technique. I learned very quickly that once I knocked on a door or rang the bell, I needed to step back several feet to wait for a response. When the door creaked open, my appearance didn't startle as many people if I just left a little more space between us before I moved in and began my pitch. I always started out by introducing myself as Joel Sonnenberg. And that I represented the Black Mountain Primary School. Then I explained that we were selling wrapping paper and assorted Christmas gifts—something everyone would soon be needing—to raise money for our PTO. So if they bought these items from us, they'd be getting something they could use and helping our school at the same time.

But the real clincher usually came when I'd tell them that if they bought something from me, it would help me reach my goal of becoming the number one salesman at Black Mountain Primary. "Then I'll win a brand-new bike!"

I had two whole sheets of orders the very first day. No one else had more than one. But the contest had a long way to go, so I was out again the next night selling more. Before the campaign ended, I think I knocked on every door in Montreat. When I ran out of houses, I went through the college dorms. Since Dad was a professor, most of the students already knew who I was. "Hey, Joel. Come on in. Whatcha got?" I'd explain, and some of the college kids even helped me make more sales to their roommates and friends. "Hey, guys, let's help Joel win a bike!"

The final tally wasn't even close. I sold almost half again as much as the second-place finisher. That gorgeous red bike was mine. Mr. Green held a big presentation ceremony in front of the whole school. I got my picture in the paper and everything.

I was so proud. It was the first time I ever got my picture in the paper for something other than the accident and being burned. I determined it wouldn't be the last.

Chapter 11

I think seeing how hard I worked for that bike reinforced in my parents' minds something they had always believed: that one of the best strategies for raising children and keeping them out of trouble was to keep them busy. They soon put that theory to the test with me.

I didn't know any grade school kids with a busier schedule than mine. Of course, schoolwork was always one priority. We also did a lot of things I was expected to participate in as a member of the Sonnenberg family. Soon after we moved to North Carolina we began attending the Montreat Presbyterian Church, which met for worship in the college chapel. As active participants we were there every Sunday morning, Sunday evening, and whenever else there was something special planned for families or children or youth.

I also got into scouting after we moved to Montreat. Ryan's mom, Mrs. Councill, was our Cub Scout den mother. So I did the Pinewood Derby, went on overnight campouts, and earned the necessary badges to begin moving up in the scouting ranks. Learning my knots was particularly difficult for me. I knew what to do; I just couldn't do it with my right hand. But I eventually demonstrated enough of the required skills to earn my knots badge.

Mom thought all children needed a chance to develop their musical gifts. So when she signed my sisters up for piano lessons, I got them too. I mastered chopsticks and a couple other numbers, and I learned to read musical notations. But like most small boys, I hated being stuck indoors to practice. And I had a better excuse than most: since I'd never be able to play more than three notes at once, I quickly realized there was no great future for me as a pianist. So Mom agreed to let me drop out of the lessons after a year. "At least you tried," she told me. "That's the important thing."

I was much more willing to "try" in other activities where I showed more potential. Like soccer—which continued to be my favorite participation sport. I might not have had much in the way of fingers and toes, but I had strong legs. I could run. And I could kick.

I remember playing a game in Asheville the first year or so we lived in North Carolina. I broke loose for a shot in front of the goal and just blasted a kick right at the net. One of the opposing players instinctively reached out with his hand to stop the shot, and it fractured his arm. I felt bad for the kid, but I didn't understand why the ref didn't award me the goal or at least give me a penalty kick for use of hands in the box.

Ryan played on the same soccer team with me. So our friendship continued to develop and grow from our interactions at practice and in games as well.

My parents encouraged my relationship with Ryan. They liked him and his family. So did I. But managing to get together wasn't always easy. The Councills lived down in Black Mountain, several miles away. It wasn't as though we could walk over to each other's house after school each day. We had to be content with time spent together in class, at Scouts, and during soccer practices and games. Or we had to arrange for our parents to drive us to each other's houses on the weekends.

Ryan was easy company. We built forts in his backyard and explored the woods and went rock hoppin' in nearby creeks during the summer. When he came to my house, we often walked up to the campus to swim in the college pool—usually buying a supply of Sugar Daddies at the candy store on the way home.

We always managed to have fun together—whether we were outside launching our G.I. Joes into the air on bottle rockets (we had to quit when our action figures lost too many limbs) or whether we were inside playing the newest Nintendo game.

I know now that video games can have negative effects on a kid's socialization process. It's possible to be so involved with virtual characters on screen that you become uninvolved in real life. But for me video games weren't so much a barrier as they were a bridge to relationships with my peers.

Because sports often serve as the social laboratory for boys growing up, I was at a real physical disadvantage when it came to playing baseball in the backyard or skateboarding down the street with my friends. But I could master any video sport. Indeed, whenever I trounced my friends at video games I wasn't above a little trash-talking to rub it in. "Ever been beat by a guy with no fingers?" Or, "I've got no hands; what's your excuse?" So video games not only provided a competitive outlet in which I could both prove myself to, and interact with, friends; they also gave me a sense of mastery that boosted my self-esteem.

I've always been a very competitive individual. If I hadn't been burned in that accident, I would have been the kind of kid who played every sport in season. I inherited not only the interest in sports but my athletic ability from my father, who'd been invited to try out for the Buffalo Bills after college but went to grad school instead.

I love to play games. I like to win. I have this intense inner drive to test my physical limits, to measure my ability to perform against myself and against others. Video games were a great outlet for that. They provided a level playing field on which I could face my friends—and beat them more often than not.

While my parents recognized and encouraged my interest in fun and games and friends, they also wanted me to learn the meaning and reward of hard work. Since they didn't foresee a lot of likely job opportunities for a nine-year-old kid like me, Mom and Dad took matters into their own hands and bought the Dairy King in downtown Black Mountain the spring of my third-grade year.

Dad planned that we'd run it as a seasonal family business during the summer, when Black Mountain attracted its fair share of tourists in search of cooler weather in the Carolina highlands. Not only would running an ice cream shop give me work experience; it would also keep me too busy to get into trouble, while at the same time providing me with spending money and maybe even a boost to my college savings account.

Of course the Dairy King offered the same benefits for my sisters as it did for me. We all worked there.

My job was to be the up-front guy—which forced me to meet the public and cope with their reactions every day. I manned the counter, greeting customers, writing down orders, taking money, working the cash register, and making change. I even had my own personal little side business selling baseball cards that I bought wholesale and sold retail.

Serving the public can be an interesting experience. But it's also work. Hard enough work that our whole family was always glad to see Labor Day come so we could close up shop until the next summer.

While every fall meant the return to school, there was more time then for friends and outdoor activities than there ever was during the summer. Mountain bikes were big among my friends. And for good reason. They were a lot more practical around Montreat than my hard-earned red coaster bike, which still looked as snazzy as ever but often had to be pushed up slopes my friends climbed with ease in low gear.

I talked to Dad about my interest in getting my own mountain bike. He wasn't so sure I could handle both the gears and the hand brakes with my right hand. I had to admit he had a point after one memorable experience borrowing a friend's bike.

After one quick lesson in how to shift, riding up to the top of our street proved to be no problem at all. The gears enabled me to do what I'd never been able to do before. Coming down presented more of a challenge. The plan was for me to coast halfway down the hill, build up a lot of speed, and then swing sharply into our driveway, letting the steep uphill pitch gradually slow me to a manageable stop.

It was a fine plan.

The only problem was that by the time I got a third of the way down the street I was already going so fast there was no way I could make the turn without splattering myself on the stone pillars on the sides of our driveway. Did I say "the only problem"? There were more. I was picking up speed at such a rate I figured I'd be doing thirty to forty miles per hour by the time I reached the T with the main road at the bottom of the hill. There was no way to steer and brake at the same time with my right hand. And there was no safe place to run off the road because the street was lined by woods.

As I approached our driveway on the right at what was literally breakneck speed, in the trees on the left side of the road I spotted the slightest of openings where a narrow footpath entered the woods at what looked to be a negotiable angle. I didn't even have time to consider the consequences. I barely had time to turn, sail off the road, and plunge into a green gauntlet of branches and limbs that slapped and lashed and whipped me all over as I fought to stay upright and spot what larger dangers lay ahead. I never did see what I hit. But the front end of the bike came to a sudden stop. And I didn't.

One second I was flipping over the handlebars and the next second I was somehow rocketing through the air with the bike flying in tight formation right behind me—only to end up on my back in a blackberry patch with the bicycle on top of me. I have no idea how long I lay there. I was still trying to determine if I'd lost any essential parts when I heard my friend running along the trail. "Joel? Where are you? Is my bike okay?"

More okay than I was. By the time I had extricated myself and my buddy's precious bike out of the blackberry brambles I looked like I'd been mauled by a herd of angry housecats. I had scratches in places I didn't know I had places. But I was all in one piece. And I had a new understanding of the challenge mountain biking held for me.

Fortunately for me, my dad also likes a challenge. He was convinced that someone somewhere must have figured out a way to mountain bike without hand brakes. And he was determined to find that someone.

I think he went to every bike shop in Asheville to explain the problem. We needed a mountain bike with gears that worked in conjunction with coaster brakes. Someone finally said he thought some German company had engineered just such a bike. Dad contacted them, and, sure enough, they had a five-speed mountain bike with coaster brakes.

It wasn't cheap. But Dad got it for me. And I spent years riding that machine for miles and miles up and down some of the most rugged off-road trails in the Smokies.

Sometimes I think the closer you live to nature and the more time you spend in the great outdoors, the more cyclical life begins to feel. It seemed that way in Montreat. Another school year meant a return of familiar faces and activities. Soccer season. Scouts. One more first-place finish in the annual PTO Christmas fund-raiser. Winters meant a peaceful stillness without the mobs of visitors— even if an occasional bear returned to rattle and roll our garbage cans in the dead of night. By the end of the school year it was time to open the Dairy King for yet another busy summer. With just enough time off for our annual family trek back to New York and the familiar sights and sounds of CAMP-of-the-WOODS— which never seemed to change.

Despite the repetitive cycle of the seasons, our life in Montreat did slowly but surely change. Third grade. Fourth grade. Fifth grade. Sixth grade. Of course I grew. So did my sisters. As did our family in February of 1990.

I'd been bugging my parents for a brother since I was five. It seemed every friend I ever had also had a brother he goofed around with. I remember pleading, "Mom, I want a brother. Everyone has one—Seth, Griff, Matt, Ryan, Johnny—I mean everyone has a brother but me."

"You better start praying then, Joel," my mother explained, "because only God is going to give you that. Your mom is just too tired to think about having another baby."

I prayed for seven years. And God finally answered—with Kyle. And I thought he was wonderful. Neither Jami nor I could ever hold him enough. My only disappointment was that I had to wait until he was two before we could start having wrestling matches.

Before Kyle was born we bought a house and moved—a short way down the mountain on the same street—into an old, rambling, two-story home we christened "Sunnymount" (the literal meaning of Sonnenberg). It had been lived in by former missionaries to China, who retired in Montreat years ago. That was one reason Ruth Graham stopped by with a housewarming gift and told us what she remembered about the house and her family's missionary friends who'd lived there.

Just as our family's growth required changes in each of our lives, my own physical growth necessitated further medical treatment. But instead of quarterly trips to the hospital, like I'd endured earlier, I averaged maybe one operation a year after we moved to Montreat. A couple more operations on my eyelids. My upper lip lowered, my mouth widened in proportion to my face, and four crowded teeth removed all at one time. Plus, they cut into the scar tissue of my wrist to give me a greater range of motion.

While that sounds like a lot, my medical care consumed less of my time each year. What's more, we began going to the Shriners Hospital in Cincinnati, which was not only closer but had a remarkably family-friendly atmosphere.

On the whole, I would have to say that our move to a "small rural community" like Montreat accomplished even more than my parents had hoped. It improved and enriched my life in unexpected ways.

As odd as it may seem to say it, moving to this tiny, sheltered, predominantly Christian community (sheltered literally by the mountains around it, sheltered socially and spiritually from the changing values in American society) in many ways expanded my personal world—which better equipped me to face the world at large.

Let me explain. Ever since the accident, I have felt like I live two lives. In two different worlds.

One is my comfortable world of home and family, where the people who know and love me most accept me for who I am inside and out. My family—not only my parents but my sisters Jami and Sommer and eventually my little brother Kyle—not only accepted my differences; they embraced them—along with the rest of me. So I could always be myself at home because I feel safe, even normal, there. My entire family always demonstrated such creative acceptance of me that "different" became "normal" at our house.

At home in this comfortable world, I can look in the mirror every morning and not feel alien. I can forget that I don't have fingers. I can take for granted who I am and accept who I am because I am accepted there. Sure, there are small reminders of reality from time to time. I can't open a can of tuna or tie my own tie. But I'm comfortable in my personal world. There are few surprises because it's very much a controlled environment.

> *My entire family always demonstrated such creative acceptance of me that "different" became "normal" at our house.*

Over the years my parents worked relentlessly to expand my safe, personal world beyond our home and family to include school. As a result of their efforts, and with the help of caring teachers and administrators along with medical professionals, I often felt that same sense of safety and acceptance in a classroom among my peers. Home and school made up the comfortable world where I lived one of my lives.

Whenever I ventured beyond the boundaries of home or school, reality kicked in. The best way to describe this reality is to say it was about as comfortable as finding myself stark naked in a world where everyone else is clothed from the Gap.

Whether I went to the mall with my family, tried to enjoy a playground at a nearby park, or even went back to the hospital for another procedure, I was bombarded with subtle glances, endless stares, and whispered comments. Little children, and sometimes even adults, would walk up to me and touch my arm or my face. Trying to tell if I was real.

It didn't matter what I was doing. I could be doing nothing. Just by being out in the real world, I elicited two basic reactions. First, I attracted unwanted attention—from innocent but curious children, from rude people who stared and pointed and whispered, even from well-meaning strangers who expressed concern at the same time their faces and eyes were broadcasting their pity. Second, in contrast to those who were drawn to me were others so repulsed and put off by me that they made cruel comments, turned away, or simply ignored me.

Both reactions pained me. Both reactions said, "You're different. You don't belong here." Both reactions happened every time I walked out of my house. There was no predicting when or where. I had to learn to live with the fact that I had no control over other people's reactions. And I wondered if I would ever feel comfortable living in the real world.

The "sheltered" community of Montreat enriched and enlarged my life by providing an expanded comfort zone and serving as a broader beachhead from which I could sortie out into the cold, uncomfortable world. I was no longer known and accepted only at home and school. For the first time in my life I had a community where people whose names I couldn't always remember smiled and said "Hi, Joel" when they encountered me around town and who never looked twice when I whizzed by on my bike.

Our move to Montreat may have done more to prepare me for the world than anything my parents ever planned for me. It helped connect the two lives I live. It was safe. It was comfortable. It was home.

Chapter 12

Middle school proved to be a fairly easy transition because the cast, the characters, and the setting remained much the same. Not only was the Sonnenberg family now firmly rooted in Montreat, but most of my classmates at Black Mountain Primary moved right along with me to Black Mountain Middle School, only a couple of blocks away.

Since I knew most of the kids in the school already and most of them knew me, my parents didn't feel the same need to "prepare" the other students for my arrival with any sort of special assembly or video introduction. Mom did, however, visit Black Mountain Middle before school started to talk to the administrators and teachers about any adjustments that might present a special challenge for me as I began sixth grade.

There was some concern about how I would deal with the locker system. Would I even be able to open my locker? As in most schools, the lockers were designed to be opened by inserting one finger into a hook-shaped latch and lifting it up. Of course, I didn't have any fingers. And the thumb and the pad on my right hand were enough bigger than an average finger that there was a question as to whether or not I could release the latch. And even if I could manage to open and close my locker, would I be able to deposit books for one subject and get all the material for my next subject in the time allotted between classes?

So Mom drove me to the school a few days before my sixth-grade year began for a trial run. The combination lock was no problem. And with a little practice I could also work the latch. Even so, for the first few days of the school year, a minute or two before the end-of-class bell sounded, my teachers would let me go to my locker, accompanied by another student to help if needed. But I managed the book exchange all by myself, so from then on I stayed in class until the bell rang and then battled the usual hallway madness, just like everyone else.

Feeling accepted by peers, finding a sense of belonging, discovering where you fit in and how you relate to the world around you, are all major concerns for most middle schoolers. My own pursuit of those goals began from a foundation of familiar activities and relationships begun in grade school and simply carried over to my junior high days.

I exercised my skills as a door-to-door salesman in a couple more PTO fund-raising campaigns during my middle school years. I can't remember any prizes I received; certainly nothing motivated me the way that red bicycle had in third grade. So the recognition and approval I received from that must have been more important in middle school than it had been at Black Mountain Primary.

Soccer continued to offer an athletic outlet and a chance to build respect and relationships as part of a team. While soccer may have been outranked by the sports of football and basketball in terms of prestige garnered by participants, it remained my sport. Since I'd played in our park recreational league every year during elementary school, Mom and Dad, along with a few other parents, decided it was time for our middle school to have its own soccer team. We raised money for uniforms and started the first-ever soccer team for Black Mountain's Owen Middle School. So it was a thrill to take the field that first season, knowing we had literally earned the uniforms we wore to represent our school on the soccer field for the first time in history.

Each summer, our family continued to operate the Black Mountain Dairy King—the benefits of which included not only pretty decent money for a summer job but bosses with the understanding and flexibility to give my sisters and me enough time off to participate in a growing number of summer camp experiences, as well as to do family activities like the annual trek back to New York for our traditional week at CAMP-of-the-WOODS.

My continuing involvement in Boy Scouts also greatly enriched my life during those middle school years. There were regular meetings and frequent overnight campouts in the Smokies at Camp Daniel Boone, where we swam in a lake that was sometimes so cold it could make your nose bleed. But my greatest scouting highlights came during special summer camps.

One year, all of us in Troop 52 earned our sailing badges during a week of living aboard a sailboat on Kentucky Lake. We had mixed feelings about our assignment to *Big Bertha*, the largest boat in the fleet. We had more room to eat our meals and to roll our sleeping bags out on the deck every night. And that deck provided a higher platform from which to jump and dive into the lake. But our size and weight made *Big Bertha* harder to maneuver than some of the smaller and lighter craft. We always seemed to be the last boat to start moving whenever the fleet hoisted sails; and once we got underway, *Big Bertha* also took longer to turn.

One morning, to get her out of a small cove where we'd anchored for the night, we tied a bunch of life jackets to a bowline, jumped in the water, and used those life jackets like harnesses to tow *Big Bertha* away from the sheltered shoreline. When we got her to deeper water, she caught a breeze, and we were finally underway.

Can you imagine it? A bunch of young teenage boys commanding their very own homely yacht. We were out in the middle of a huge lake—swimming, laughing, and eating. At night, with the vast starry sky stretched out like a dark canopy over us, we would lie on our backs on the deck, looking up with breathtaking wonder at the universe on display above what suddenly seemed like a very tiny craft. With the gentle rocking of the sailboat and the waves slightly lapping at its sides, all seemed right with God, the universe, and the world that I was in. Could it get any better than this? I had become captain of my own vessel. But I could only steer. I would be dead in the water without the wind powering my sails. Though still a mere teenager, I was becoming a young man with questions of my own. What lay ahead for me? If it was anything like my previous years, it would be full of excitement and adventure. One thing was certain: I knew Who powered my sails. And I was having a blast!

I think the last day on Kentucky Lake was the most memorable. After a week of little wind, we finally got a stiff breeze. When we hoisted our sails and caught a gust, we had to take back every ugly thing we'd said and thought about *Big Bertha*. With her sails full and our crew cheering, *Big Bertha* sprinted through the rest of the scout fleet as though they were standing still. What a way to end an unforgettable week!

Dad was always involved with me in Scouts. So he shared a number of camping adventures and even played a very significant role in the earning of a badge one year at Camp Ho Non Wah. During that camp I informed my father that I wanted to earn my shotgun badge. But like many things in life for me, it wasn't that simple.

I'd already completed my gun safety training and had earned my marksmanship badge on a rifle range. But shooting clay pigeons with a shotgun was an entirely different challenge. A rifle is fairly short; I could rest the stock and barrel on my stump of my left arm, hold the rifle steady, and pull the trigger with my right hand. Not only was a shotgun longer and heavier than a target rifle, but shooting clay pigeons meant swinging the gun to follow the six-inch clay discs as they sailed through the air.

As Dad and I watched some of the other scouts shoot, I realized there was no way I could hold the barrel of the shotgun and swing the muzzle to follow the flight of the clay pigeons. "My left arm is too short to shoot that way," I told my dad.

We watched for a while longer. "Maybe if I could rest the barrel on your arm I could follow the flight of the disc by swinging the butt end of the gun," I concluded.

"We can try," Dad replied.

We walked over to explain what we were thinking to the instructor, who quickly okayed the plan. "As long as you're just resting the muzzle on your dad's arm and you're doing the aiming and the shooting," he told me, "that will work for me."

So we took our positions, and I yelled out that I was ready. Phfffft. The first clay pigeon went sailing. The target broke into bits on launch, so I aimed at one of the biggest pieces as it sailed off to the left. BOOM! The fragment shattered. "WOW!" I could tell Dad and the scoutmaster in charge of the range thought it was just plain luck. So I got set for another shot and yelled, "Ready!" Phfffft! Boom!

"Ready!" Phfffft! Boom! "Ready!" Phfffft! Boom!

I hit thirteen out of fifteen targets. After a short break, I took a longer turn and hit something like forty-one out of forty-five targets—more than enough to qualify for my shotgun badge. I guess all those years of playing video games were finally paying off.

I don't think the instructor believed it. Even my father acted impressed. "Your turn!" I grinned, as I handed him the shotgun.

Dad laughed and shook his head. "No way!" I guess I'd whipped him one too many times at Pac-Man. He refused to even try.

My biggest scouting adventure of all was the Boy Scouts of America Jamboree outside of Washington, D.C., the summer after my seventh-grade year.

Dad didn't go with me. But Ryan did. Along with twenty thousand or so of our closest friends from all over the United States.

Mom worried about me camping for eight days in an open field under a scorching midsummer sun. She sent a letter to the organizers explaining that, because I had no sweat glands on any of the burned portions of my body, I could be very susceptible to heatstroke. So, as a necessary safety precaution, it was imperative that arrangements be made for me (and my friend Ryan) to go swimming every afternoon during the hottest part of the day.

The scout leaders said that would be no problem. And they were as good as their word. Each afternoon Ryan and I caught a bus that dropped us off at a nearby pool and came back to pick us up a couple of hours later. What a deal! Not only were we able to take a refreshing dip each day while our friends were sweltering back at camp; we signed up for lessons at the pool and earned our scuba diving badge before the jamboree ended.

My previous sales experience served me well at the jamboree. One of scouting's traditions at national events is trading troop badges. I started out with eight of ours, and before I was done, I'd collected dozens of badges of different troops from as far away as Arizona and Alaska. I did so well at trading that my campmates would give me their badges and ask me (on their behalf) to trade for as many different emblems as possible. I had fun and got to meet a lot of people in the process.

My parents' belief that keeping kids busy goes a long way toward keeping them out of trouble continued to be true for me. I didn't go through that early adolescent rebellion so common at junior high age. Nor did I repeat the peer-pressure mistakes I'd made when we first moved to Montreat.

The only serious mischief I got into during middle school was completely unintentional and not really any doing of mine. One day a friend I'll call Sam and I decided to hike over to the Montreat campus to shoot baskets on one of the outdoor courts. We were walking along a wooded trail behind some nearby houses when I noticed my buddy had stopped. I turned around and went back to find Sam bent over a tree stump at the edge of one of the backyards.

"What are you doing?" By the time I finished asking the question, he'd turned enough for me to see he was trying to light a firecracker with a match.

"Hey, don't do that!" I said.

"It won't light anyway," Sam complained, dropping the match and turning away to walk in my direction. When he marched right past me, I pivoted and followed along behind him toward the campus.

A short while later one of our friends came walking out on the court where we were shooting hoops. "Did you guys hear the fire trucks?" he wanted to know.

"Where were they going?"

When he told us the name of the street, my heart sank.

"Let's go see!" Sam insisted. I didn't really want to go. But I felt I had no choice.

I could smell the smoke even before I could see the firefighters through the trees—rolling up their hose and hauling their other gear back to their truck. From a familiar stump near the trail in the edge of the woods all the way to the house, everything was charred black. The fire had consumed the entire backyard, including all the grass and a few bushes and small trees. I could even see where the flames had begun to scorch the siding on the back of the house before the firefighters had put them out.

I knew good and well how the fire had started, but I wondered how much the firefighters could figure out. So I walked over to the nearest firefighter and asked, "What happened?"

"Somebody prob'ly dropped a cigarette," he said. "Happens all the time. Thisun coulda been serious. Another five minutes and that house woulda caught on fire."

I heard the guy out and then watched the firefighters finish cleaning up, hoping I didn't look as guilty as I felt. As we walked away and headed home a few minutes later, my insides were churning with mixed feelings. Relieved there was no permanent damage, glad that evidently no one had seen us earlier, real regret about our responsibility, and shame that we hadn't spoken up and admitted what had happened. I told myself I wasn't the one with the matches. That was true. I told myself no lasting damage was done. That, too, was true. I also told myself that if I were to confess what had happened, Sam would be in a lot more trouble than I would. So I decided to keep my mouth shut.

For a long time I couldn't help feeling guilty about my silence. But whenever I thought about it, the memory of that incident, added to my earlier vandalism experience, served as a warning to me about my friendships. Getting in with the wrong crowd could be like playing with fire; if you weren't careful, you could get in trouble just by being in the wrong place at the wrong time.

C h a p t e r 1 3

T hankfully, Ryan and I still had each other. After sharing classes, soccer, and scouting experiences during our primary school years, our friendship was a big part of the "foundation" I took with me into junior high. Without ever really talking about it, I guess we both tested the waters with other relationships when we first got to middle school. We met new kids. And we each made new friends. But I think those experiences and friendships with other people soon served to strengthen the bond between us by reminding us of how well we complemented each other and how much we had in common.

Our families had become close over the years. Not only had Mrs. Councill been our den mother back in Cub Scouts, but Ryan's dad and my dad were both leaders of our Boy Scout troop. So our parents observed and encouraged our friendship. Everyone believed we were good for each other. And I thought they were right.

For one thing, Ryan and I were both homebodies. Ryan was shy. And for reasons I've already talked about, I still didn't think it was fun to go out in public all the time. So we didn't go to many parties. Nor did we hang out at the mall like a lot of our friends did. We had more fun at home playing games, watching videos, swimming in his pool, or just hanging out.

When I did venture out in public as a young teenager, most of the attention I drew seemed a little more subtle and low-key than it had been in my younger days. Not as many little kids would touch my hands or my face. And not nearly as many adults would make a point to speak to me.

Sure, just as many people stared at me. And I occasionally resorted to a frequently funny but not necessarily kind or sensitive response. When I went shopping at the mall or somewhere else, I'd sometimes notice a group of younger kids tagging along behind—just watching me and waiting to see what happened. Usually I ignored them and went about my business. But if they got too annoying, or if I just wasn't in the mood to be gawked at, I might suddenly turn around and walk toward my followers. When they hurried away, I'd follow them, just like they had followed me. Sometimes they would scatter and run. Other times they would duck into a store and try to lose me amidst alternate aisles and clothes racks.

I wanted them to learn better manners, but even if they didn't, I hope they got an unpleasant sense of what it felt like to be stalked. At the very least, I know I received a little mischievous pleasure when, after years of stares and finger-pointing, I turned the tables and took control of an unpleasant situation.

Most of the time my response to the world around me was more positive and productive. I didn't merely cling to old relationships and the same activities I'd tried in the past. Like most kids, I saw middle school as a chance to spread my wings and try new things, explore new activities.

Like band. Because it was a big deal at Black Mountain Middle School, I decided to give it a try. It didn't really matter that I had no mastery of any musical instrument. No one in sixth-grade beginning band did. We were all pretty much in the same boat. Almost.

I knew from my experience with recorders in elementary school music classes that I would never be any good on a woodwind instrument. I didn't have enough fingers to cover the holes for various notes. My lack of lips, as well as fingers, pretty much eliminated the brass instruments. The only real option available to me in band was percussion, so I became a drummer.

I enjoyed my band experience. My classmates and I learned together. The simple rhythms proved to be no problem. But I quickly realized there was very little future for a one-handed drummer. So I dropped out of band after one year and turned to chorus as my primary creative musical outlet during seventh and eighth grade.

What started out as a musical experiment turned into a truly great experience. We had a lot of fun in chorus. Not just learning the music but competing in festivals as well. It wasn't until years later that I learned that many, if not most, serious burn survivors suffer extensive smoke and heat damage to their larynx, throat, and lungs. As a result, some of them have little or no voice left. Incredibly, I had no such injuries, despite my extensive burns. I could speak normally. I even won all-state honors in middle school chorus. I could breathe as easily and yell as loudly as anyone on the soccer field. And for all of that, I've learned to be eternally grateful.

Just as I had experimented and tried out my options in music during middle school, I took a similar approach to sports. Soccer remained a given. But I itched to measure myself against my peers in other competitive sports as well.

Football was never a real possibility. Growing up I enjoyed the occasional game of touch football in the backyard. I'd play catch and run simulated pass patterns during recess. I surprised a lot of people by how accurate a spiral I could throw. But I knew there was no way, even with protective pads and a helmet, that I could ever withstand the rigors of middle school tackle football.

Basketball presented a whole different set of challenges. But it's such a huge sport in North Carolina—and so many of my friends played—that I decided to go with Ryan and a number of our buddies when they signed up for the week-long Brad Dougherty Basketball Camp during the summer between my seventh- and eighth-grade years. Brad Dougherty had grown up locally and been a big college star at the University of North Carolina before going on to become a perennial NBA All-Star with the Cleveland Cavaliers. So this camp, too, was a big deal—with a couple hundred campers who attended.

Most people are surprised at how well I shoot a basketball. I play a pretty mean game of H-O-R-S-E—as long as I don't have to make any left-handed trick shots. So I did fairly well in the shooting drills we ran at camp.

My biggest bugaboo was dribbling. I only had the one hand, so I almost always had to go to my right. And the fact that my right hand didn't have fingers made it tough to maintain much control of my dribble, no matter which way I went with the ball. So whenever we scrimmaged, I told myself, *Just play defense! Don't worry about scoring. Forget dribbling. Just don't let your man get free, and never let him get a shot off without a hand in his face.*

You don't have to dribble to play defense. You just have to be quick, consistent, and committed to sticking to your man. I could do that. Whomever I was assigned to guard, I was on 'em like glue, always staying between my man and the goal or between my man and the ball, swatting passes away, sticking my hand in his face every time he even thought about shooting.

Evidently that effort was noticed. Our local Owen High School basketball coach attended camp one afternoon. I assumed he was there to check out the up-and-coming middle school talent to get an idea as to which of my friends he could count on to be playing varsity ball in a few years. Since basketball had never been my sport, I didn't have any such aspirations. So it came as a complete shock to me when the coach pulled me aside after one of our scrimmage sessions to tell me how impressed he was by my defense. "If you want to play for me when you get to high school, Joel," he assured me, "I'll make a place for you on the varsity. We can always use that kind of effort."

I couldn't believe what I was hearing. I thanked the coach for his complimentary words. But I remember thinking, *I'm not really that good!* I could believe he'd noticed my hard work and appreciated the effort. But the part about him saving me a spot on the varsity if I wanted it? That was a bit much. I figured he was impressed by what I could do, given my physical limitations, but I had no aspirations of becoming the first fingerless Globetrotter.

However, another occurrence that week got me thinking that maybe there was more to it. The last day in the afternoon we sat on the court for the camp's official awards ceremony. Brad Dougherty reviewed some of what we had covered and thanked us for participating. Then after he called us one at a time to hand out our participation certificates, he announced that he had a few special awards to give out. He passed out trophies for various offensive and defensive accomplishments. Everyone applauded the recipients as they walked down front to receive the awards, get another handshake, and have their picture taken with the towering Cavalier center.

I thought he was done, when he announced there was one more very special award that went to a camper demonstrating courage, character, effort—I don't remember all of what Brad talked about, until he got to the final part where he said, "This year's 'Toughest Kid in Camp' award, along with a gift certificate for an authentic Reebok warm-up suit, goes to . . . Joel Sonnenberg." I guess everyone applauded as I jumped to my feet and wove my way through the crowd to the front. I was more focused on the trophy and the gift certificate for the cool warm-ups than on the recognition of my fellow campers. But at the same time I remembered the exchange I'd had earlier with the Owen High School basketball coach, and I thought, *This has been some week!*

After that experience I considered going out for the middle school basketball team my eighth-grade year. But then I thought better of it. I really didn't think I was that good. And there were plenty of other things for me to do.

Among the new opportunities that came my way during my middle school years was the chance to share my story publicly with others. I'd appeared on television numerous times when I was little. And I'd made a bunch of appearances with Mom during the publicity tour for her book. But she and Dad had done almost all the talking; I'd usually just walk out, say a couple of words, and wave to the crowd.

Now I was old enough to speak for myself. And one of the first opportunities I received was an invitation to appear on *The Maury Povich Show*. My parents and I flew to New York for the taping. During the show, Maury Povich summarized the story of the accident and told viewers about all the medical procedures and operations I'd been through. We talked a little about school, scouting, soccer, and other activities I was involved in. And, like most adults do when talking to kids, he asked me about my plans for the future. All in all I felt the program went pretty well.

Of course, I had to get special permission to be excused from school to tape the show, so the principal insisted on knowing when the program would air. Then he made arrangements for all the classes in the entire school to see it.

I remember sitting in the darkened library with a bunch of my seventh-grade classmates as *The Maury Povich Show* came on the television our librarian had set up for us. I already felt self-conscious just knowing the whole school would be watching. Then everyone applauded when I appeared on the screen.

As I watched the interview proceed on the screen, if I could have crawled under my chair or, better yet, snuck out of that library never to return to middle school, I would have done it.

I could not believe that I'd felt good about the program at the end of the taping. I hemmed and hawed and said "and uh . . ." so many times it was painful to watch. I didn't remember feeling particularly nervous on the set when we'd taped the show. But the Joel Sonnenberg on the television screen in that middle school library looked and acted terrified.

Everyone around me seemed engrossed by the show. And afterward teachers and students made a point of telling me how much they enjoyed the program, how well I'd done, and so on. But all I could think of was how nervous I'd looked, how inarticulate I'd been. Even as the people around me praised my performance,

I dismissed their opinions and told myself, *I am never going to embarrass myself by acting that nervous ever again!*

One wonderful thing did come out of that embarrassing television appearance. Because I wore a Duke basketball sweatshirt for the taping of the show, Maury Povich commented on my attire. This was the year after Coach Mike Krzyzewski's team had won the national championship, so I explained that I was a huge fan of the Blue Devils. Maury asked if I went to many of their games. When I admitted I'd never had the privilege of attending a Duke basketball game, he said that maybe something could be arranged. But after the conversation moved on to another topic, I never gave his comment any further serious consideration.

A few months later we received a long-distance phone call from Durham. Evidently some big Blue Devil booster had seen the show, heard me say I'd love to go see a game, and either sent a tape of the show to Coach K or at least told him my story. Now Coach K's secretary was calling to invite me to attend any Duke game during the 1991–92 season. My choice.

I picked a big nonconference game at home against Notre Dame. Coach K not only provided tickets for me, my parents, my sisters Jami and Sommer, and my cousin BJ, but he also sent a white stretch limo to pick us up at our hotel, drive us to campus, and deliver us right to the door of the school's Cameron Indoor Stadium.

A Duke official escorted us right past the students who'd been camping on the lawn, waiting in line for tickets for two weeks. He walked us right inside with the rest of the Cameron Crazies and led us to our reserved seats in the first row behind the Duke bench. I couldn't believe this was really happening.

I was even more amazed during the pregame hoopla, with the fans already screaming and rocking the building, when one of the security men caught my eye and motioned for me to follow him. We slipped out of the gymnasium, down a tunnel, along a short corridor, past several security men, and through a door. Suddenly we were standing in the Duke locker room. "Hi, Joel!" Coach K walked over to greet me and shake my hand. Then he introduced me to the team— Christian Laettner, Bobby Hurley, Grant Hill, and all my other heroes. I got to stay in the locker room for Coach's last-minute instructions to the team and then hurried back to the stands just in time for the team's entrance and the opening ceremonies.

"Where have you been?" Dad leaned forward to ask. I thought he'd seen me being escorted out, but he evidently assumed I'd gone to the restroom or something. I turned and told him matter-of-factly, "With the team in the Duke locker room."

Dad gave me this surprised look, then a huge grin crossed his face and he just shook his head. I laughed. Now that I think about it, it seemed unbelievable to me too. But after watching and cheering the Blue Devils to another win, Dad himself got to go with me and take pictures in the victorious locker room, where Coach K actually cleared out all the reporters clamoring for postgame quotes by announcing, "We've got to talk to Joel." When it was just Dad and me and the team, Coach K asked me to give my assessment of the team's play. I told the guys they played great, then chatted one-on-one with the players, several of whom gave me souvenirs to take home—autographs, shirts, caps, even an authentic Duke basketball jersey. The coach presented me with a national championship pin. After fifteen to twenty minutes, when it was finally time to tell the team good-bye and I'd thanked Coach K for a wonderful afternoon, he invited me back again the following season. "Any game, any place, Joel," he said. "Just call and tell me when."

I assured him I would do it. That was a promise I intended to keep.

To top off what had been one of the most memorable days of my life, my family all watched the eleven o'clock news that evening on Durham's WTVD. The broadcast led off with a story about my attendance at the game. They'd assigned a Channel 11 reporter and a camera crew to interview us and follow me around all afternoon. So the whole family was curious to see what kind of story they had put together.

The news anchor introduced the piece as a "stuff of dreams" story about a young North Carolina boy. He said, "Joel Sonnenberg isn't your typical fourteen-year-old." He called me "a fighter" and explained very briefly about the accident, my injuries, and the long recovery road. They showed videotape of us getting out of the limo and being escorted into the game. They showed me in the stands cheering on the team and then meeting with the players in the locker room after the game.

They played part of a courtside interview where the reporter asked how I felt about all the special treatment. "I didn't expect anything like this," I told her. "It's wonderful. I feel like royalty or something. I feel like the future president of the United States."

They showed Christian Laettner taking one of his patented jump shots and said this player (meaning Laettner) "looked up to by so many boys says he admires this boy." Then Christian said, "Joel's just a great kid. He reminds you that, even when bad things happen to you, you can still be upbeat and positive."

"I don't think of myself as that inspirational. I see myself as a normal, everyday kid."

That's when they played another quote of me saying, "I don't think of myself as that inspirational. I see myself as a normal, everyday kid."

The story came to the end, and I thought, YES! What a great way to end the segment! In part because I wanted other people to think of me as "a normal kid," but mostly because I felt I'd come across so much better on TV. I looked like I was having fun.

And this time I didn't say "and uh . . ." even once.

Chapter 14

I guess I served as a good example of why the teenage years can be so confusing. Part of me still clung to the goal I'd grown up with. Despite the differences between me and the people around me, or perhaps because of those differences, all my life I had wanted to be seen as "a normal kid."

Yet there was another part of me—a "normal adolescent" part—that wanted to find out who I really was and what it was that made me a unique creation of God. Every day of my life since the accident I'd been reminded that I was so different I could never quite fit into any crowd as just another "normal kid." But that was all just appearance, wasn't it? Surface stuff. What about the real me? Under the scars, how much was I just like everyone else? How much was I different? Who did I truly want to be? And how do you define "normal" anyway?

I know now that these are basic youth issues. But during my teen years they were complicated and magnified for me by my experiences, my circumstances, my story.

Thankfully, I had a solid foundation to build on, a safe base camp from which to venture out in my adolescent exploration. I still had that sense of community (at home in Montreat and at school) that not only made me feel accepted but respected. I had wise parents and loving siblings who somehow affirmed both my normality and my uniqueness at the same time.

When people stared or were rude, my parents told me, "Those people just don't know you like we do." My parents, better than anyone else, remembered that, underneath the surface, I had all the normal human emotions. And in that way I was like everyone else.

Yet my parents also believed and taught my siblings and me that we were all unique creations of God. So as far back as I can remember they also convinced me I was literally one in a billion: "Because you were saved in that accident, because you lived through perhaps the worst injuries to any burn survivor in history, God must have some very special plans in store for you, Joel."

I absorbed both messages my parents tried to convey. And those beliefs influenced the basic question I was asking. Even in the early teen years I think I realized, in my heart, that the question wasn't just "Who am I?" or even "Who do I truly want to be?" The real question was "Who does God want me to be?"

The real question was "Who does God want me to be?"

That's a heavy question, whoever you are. Whenever you ask it.

I think I'd resolved most of my peer-pressure issues several years earlier. I knew after my vandalism experiences that it wasn't always a good idea to be a follower. Scouting, church, family, and all my years of school since we'd moved to Montreat combined to start me thinking, *Maybe I am cut out to be a leader.*

So I spent all four years of high school testing the idea.

As a young teenager, one of the ways I both tested and developed my leadership skills was by sharing my experience—my story—through public speaking. The summer before I started high school I was invited to speak at a Fellowship of Christian Athletes camp in Virginia. So I just told my story—summarizing the accident, telling how people had prayed for me all my life, recounting a little about my miraculous recovery, talking about the blessings and opportunities God had given me (including the visit just months before with the Duke basketball team). Then I challenged the campers to first consider how much the Lord had done in my life and then to ask themselves, *If God can do that with Joel, what can he do for me?*

I was a little surprised at the positive reactions of the camp staff, coaches, and campers (a lot of them several years older than I was) after my talk. So many of them approached me—to thank me, to say I'd inspired them, or just to wish me well.

It may have been the first time I began to realize the power of the podium. My life experience had always made me sensitive to people's reactions to me. And I'd tried to learn to accept and live with those reactions, positive or negative, because they were out of my control.

Yet it seemed that a few minutes of standing in front of people and talking about myself and my experience gave me a new measure of control. People still responded in a variety of ways—most of them positive. But there seemed to be less awkwardness—perhaps because they saw me as a person. And in all the reactions I sensed an encouraging, underlying attitude of respect.

———————

That same summer our Montreat Presbyterian youth group gave me a different kind of opportunity to make an impact on the lives of others. I had been a big fan of our new church youth director, Shawn Stewart, ever since I'd served on the committee that interviewed him for the job.

As part of that "get to know each other" process, several other members of our youth group and I went out to eat with Shawn. During dinner our conversation somehow turned to vegetables we hated. Shawn laughed and told us that eating the most repulsive vegetables was no big deal. "All you have to do is hold your nose while you do it."

No sooner had the comment come out of his mouth than he suddenly glanced at me, obviously wishing he could take back his words. "Easy for you guys!" I cracked. And everyone burst out laughing.

Later Shawn took me aside and sheepishly asked, "How long does it usually take someone to say something stupid like that?"

I grinned. "Usually not long," I responded. I not only voted to hire the guy, but from that day on I was in his corner. So when he challenged the youth of our church to make service and missions a priority, I was usually one of the first in the group to sign up for any opportunity.

That summer before my freshman year Shawn took a group of about twenty-five of us to an inner-city neighborhood in Savannah, Georgia, to spend a week building homes with Habitat for Humanity. The experience turned out to be more of an adventure than expected because our group was to spend the entire week working on roofs.

I'd never done any work like that. But I learned. I suspect some of the Habitat leaders wondered at first if I should be allowed to climb the ladder. But the fact that I had a very good sense of balance proved to be an advantage when it came to scrambling up and down steeply pitched roofs.

OUACHITA TECHNICAL COLLEGE

Nailing down shingles is pretty much a two-handed job. While I'd mastered harder tasks in my life, I quickly decided I didn't need to figure out how to position and hold a shingle while I hammered in a nail. I could be a lot more helpful—and actually improve everyone else's efficiency—by hauling bundles of shingles up to the roof and then positioning myself on the peak, where I would slide shingles down to all the other workers as they needed them. By the end of the week I'd become known as "the shingle-meister."

Not that all of my energies were devoted to such noble causes. As ninth grade began, I became pretty absorbed in North American high school life. I ran for and was elected treasurer of my freshman class. And after being named "the best junior varsity forward" that fall of my freshman year, I was already looking forward to playing a lot more varsity soccer during the remainder of my high school career.

As winter approached, I remembered the promise Owen High's basketball coach had given me during the Brad Dougherty Basketball Camp. But I decided not to take him up on his offer of a place on his squad. Instead, I went to him late that fall of my freshman year and asked if he needed a team manager. He gave me the job on the spot. Sure, it was a lot of work. But I enjoyed being part of the team—not just on game nights but on the bus, in the locker room, and at practice everyday after school.

Our youth group provided another opportunity for leadership that next summer between ninth and tenth grade when I went with about twenty young people and adult chaperones on a short-term mission trip to South America. Our team took on an assortment of construction and maintenance projects for a Christian youth camp in Bolivia. I did a variety of jobs, but my primary assignment was that of group foreman—making sure each of our working teams had the necessary manpower, equipment, and supplies to complete their tasks. I also did some speaking, using the services of a translator, when we helped lead worship.

For a month our group lived and worked alongside the Bolivians. Which gave us the time and opportunity to develop relationships with the children and teenagers around the camp and with the people in the local churches who staffed and supported this facility.

I enjoyed the friendliness and warmth of the people. But I was also a little put off by the reaction I got whenever I went out in public. Unlike in the States, people made no real attempt to disguise their curiosity. They clearly didn't consider it at all rude to stare or even point.

Most of the time I managed to ignore the unwanted attention. But I remember one evening when a bunch of us took a long walk after supper. As we walked past a street-corner flower stand, a young man selling roses began tagging along after us. Before long it became apparent to me that he wasn't so much interested in making a sale as he was in working his way up through our group to where he could get a better look at me. Every time I glanced back he was a little closer and looking toward me. I didn't say anything or acknowledge him in any way until he was right behind me. Then I whirled around, raised my arms, and bellowed out the best monster sound I could make. The poor guy screamed, "Ninja! Ninja!" and staggered into a chain-link fence before he righted himself and sprinted in the opposite direction.

It probably wasn't the most effective evangelistic technique; I never saw the guy again. But I got to know a lot of other Bolivians quite well. We saw how they lived. We visited their homes and even shared their food. And as a result of observing their lives, I came back to the States with a new perspective on my lifestyle. Even after I began my sophomore year of high school back in North Carolina, my ongoing concern for my new Bolivian friends prompted me to help start a drive at church to raise money for a new kitchen at the youth camp where our mission team had worked.

As a sophomore, in addition to my involvement in Owen High's sports programs—starting for the varsity soccer team and serving again as manager for the boys basketball team—I had been elected president of my class. My primary presidential duty, other than conducting a couple of class meetings, was to plan and put on the annual sophomore-freshman dance.

I guess you could say there was a bit of irony in the fact that I was to be the main man planning one of the biggest social events of the year at Owen High School. I had never been what you would call a dating animal. In fact, I'd hardly dated at all. It wasn't the fact that I couldn't date; I just wouldn't. Instead I studied girls from a distance, biding my time for the right one to come along. Which eventually happened in tenth grade.

I hadn't really noticed her in middle school. But I definitely noticed her now. She sat right behind me in literature class. Along with a knockout smile, she had a personality that accentuated her beauty. We talked every day in class. We passed notes. Occasionally, when the teacher was lecturing in the middle of class, I would hear her giggle at something I had written. I loved that sound.

Apparently she liked the sound of spending time together outside of school. And I was more than willing to oblige. We picnicked, hiked, watched movies, and even played soccer with each other. All in all, we had a wonderful time.

Granted, most guys wait and wonder if and when the time is right to put an arm around her during a movie, when to reach out and take her hand as they walk together, when it's okay to kiss her for the first time—and how long that first kiss should be. But the truth was, I did have some unique concerns. How do you hold hands if you don't have hands? How do you go about kissing someone when you don't have lips? If I can't do the "natural" things to show her I like her, what is there to love about me?

They say that "love will find a way." And I guess it's true.

The bigger question was what to make of the new emotions I was experiencing over those first few weeks of that relationship. I'd never felt, or even imagined, anything like this.

It wasn't that I'd never felt accepted at school before. I had. But now I felt really accepted, or maybe I felt acceptable in a new way. It amazed me that the attention and affection of one cute girl could make such an impact on me. On everything!

If I can't do the "natural" things to show her I like her, what is there to love about me?

For example, my standard strategy for dealing with unwanted attention and stares had been to ignore them. There were the rare occasions when I directly countered someone's rudeness by saying something, but the vast majority of the time, I routinely ignored the daily stares and finger-pointing.

Suddenly I found I couldn't do that anymore. I couldn't just shrug off the stares and refuse to let them affect me because I wasn't just "me" anymore; I was part of "us." And in tuning in to my girlfriend's feelings, I was aware of her reactions. Even when she tried to ignore the stares, I was aware of her effort. Which made it impossible for me to ignore those stares any longer.

Even if she meant it when she said it didn't matter, I knew it did. And even if it didn't matter to her, it now did to me. Perhaps that's why, for the first time in my life, I found myself regularly looking in mirrors. I usually avoided my reflection—for obvious reasons. Mirrors reminded me of how different I was from other people. And they never accurately reflected the total image I had of myself and the person I was inside.

So I spent little time in front of a mirror, unless maybe it was to walk up behind one of my sisters and stare when she complained about an incoming pimple. "Hey, at least you can get pimples!" I would say. (Only close family members and friends knew that my scars made it physically impossible for me to get pimples.)

"You're so lucky!" my sisters would say.

"I know!" I'd grin. Minor blemishes were of no concern to me. My physical flaws were all too obvious. I hardly needed a mirror to remind me what they were.

And yet, in contrast with my previous carefree attitude, I suddenly developed this inexplicable concern about appearance now that I had a girlfriend—as if by looking in the mirror I could somehow change or improve the way I looked.

One day my sister Sommer happened to catch me evaluating my image. She stopped and caught my reflected eyes. "Hmm. You look different in a mirror, Joel," she said thoughtfully.

"What do you mean?"

"I don't know," she said. "Strange."

I laughed. "Thanks, Sommer."

She grinned. "What I meant was that your reflection just doesn't look like you. You look better in person."

"Really?" What did she mean? Why wouldn't my reflection look right to Sommer, who saw me from the outside every day?

Then it hit me. My face isn't symmetrical. No one's is perfectly symmetrical, but mine isn't even close. The left side of my face was burned much more deeply in the accident than my right.

Lots of people, when they have photographs taken, laugh and talk about their good side and their bad side—even when the difference is minuscule. I might not have a good side. But I do have a best side. It had never mattered to me before. Now it did. And in my reflection it was opposite the way other people looked at me. That's what looked "strange" to Sommer when she saw me in the mirror.

I could only hope she was right about her other assessment. That I looked better in person.

I will never know how much my appearance mattered to my first real girlfriend. There were a lot of differences between us, which I spent little energy thinking seriously about at the time. Like our backgrounds. And our values. Over time, as the differences in our values became more apparent, our relationship came to an end.

Even though that relationship had only lasted a few short months, during those glorious days she had filled my mind and my heart. She'd brought something into my life I'd never experienced before. So in the aftermath, I wondered, *Was she in it for the glamour of dating someone like me?*

It may sound absurd, but I called it part of my "celebrity status." For example, I was well-known throughout my community and school. Everywhere I went I attracted attention—good or bad. And there was a small bit of status in dating someone like me: the girl seemed to be stronger and more beautiful when she stood next to me. And I, for one, totally agreed!

But in the dating scene, all those reasons ended up being superficial. Reality proved a harder dose of medicine. It's amazing how quickly glamour fades away when you daily ask a girl to tie your shoes or put a Band-Aid over a recent cut.

Maybe she had been in the relationship for what she could get out of it or to feel better about herself.

None of this speculation did anything to improve my spirits.

Chapter 15

They say time heals all wounds. Maybe they're right. But keeping busy helps too. At least it distracts you. And there are times in life when distraction is good.

In addition to all my activities at school and church, I also had a job that sophomore year—working twelve hours a week as a dishwasher in the cafeteria at Montreat College, where my dad taught. Scraping, washing, and disinfecting dishes in any commercial kitchen is messy, smelly work. And the steamy conditions presented a special problem for me. The scar tissue covering most of my body contains no functional sweat glands, so it's easy for me to get overheated. Yet I found this work experience somehow satisfying and reassuring—I guess because it gave me the chance to prove to myself that I could handle the duties of a "normal" job as effectively as anyone else.

My ongoing relationship with my best friend, Ryan, also provided a beneficial "distraction" in the wake of my romantic breakup. He played an important role in drawing me out of my room and getting me to stop moping and start participating in life again.

Ironically, Ryan was every bit as clueless about girls as I was, even though he always had the kind of looks that turned girls' heads. And not the way I did. With both an older and a younger sister, I think I had a pretty good idea of what and who girls considered handsome. And Ryan had it all. But the poor guy was too painfully shy to know what to do with it.

I was encouraging him all the time to ask out this girl or that girl, because I could tell they were interested. But he didn't believe me. Or maybe it was because he broke out in a sweat, literally, at the thought of approaching any girl to ask her out.

So the two of us spent most of our Friday and Saturday nights together at his house or mine. Playing games, watching ball games on TV, or just hanging out.

We enjoyed each other's families. I'd call his house, and if his mom answered, I'd ask, "Is there an opening at Camp Councill tonight?" She'd laugh and say, "Sure, Joel, come on over." I was always welcome.

Ryan had two brothers and no sisters, so he appreciated the interchange with Jami and Sommer whenever he came over to our house. They accepted him as part of the family—often referring to him as "Joel's other half," or "our half brother, Ryan." But somehow our comfortable, natural, and positive interaction with my sisters (and sometimes with their friends) didn't seem to translate very successfully into other settings and other experiences Ryan and I had with members of the female gender.

We liked girls. We certainly noticed girls. We looked at girls. We even talked about girls. But that was about as far as it went most of the time.

Let me give you two examples of our "expertise" with women:

Ryan and I never did much cruising. But one night when we were out together, we pulled to a stop at a red light. A car full of teenage girls pulled up next to us. When I glanced over and made eye contact with one of them, I saw the startled look on her face as she turned away to say something to her friends. It was a familiar reaction, so I turned my attention to the light and the road ahead—instinctively avoiding the stares I knew were coming.

However, that was about the time Ryan glanced out the side window and exclaimed, "Wow! Hey, Joel! Look at those girls! I think they're scopin' me out."

I knew better. But I didn't say anything because Ryan was actually smiling and nodding at the girls by this time. And I didn't want to burst the boy's bubble.

"Did you see 'em?" Ryan wanted to know, after the girls had peeled out and left us sitting at the light. "I think they liked me." I didn't even try to explain.

I think we succeeded in making more of an impression on girls the time Ryan and I went skiing at a slope not far outside of Asheville called Hawk's Nest. Our favorite run there consisted of almost constant moguls, which gave us plenty of opportunity to show off our skiing skills.

Like most ski slopes, Hawk's Nest had one of those spots on the course where there's a bigger than usual mogul, which skiers have fashioned into a jump that provides a little more elevation and big air than the course designers planned or the course operators' liability insurer really wants you to experience. We naturally looked for that spot every time down.

I got a bit overconfident and decided to show Ryan what a real skier could do. I hit the ramp at full speed and took off in perfect form. But I went so high and far that when I landed I skidded out of control into a safety barrier with such force that I broke one of the barrels. Thankfully, the only serious damage was to my ego, so I jumped up and tried to walk off like the collision was nothing at all—just a minor, everyday occurrence for an experienced skier like me. Only to find it's impossible to act convincingly nonchalant and macho while your best friend is standing there laughing his head off at you.

I owed Ryan one. And I found the way to pay him back that very same afternoon.

All day long Ryan had been talking about this gorgeous girl he kept seeing on the slopes. "Did you see her, Joel? She is really something!" We'd be riding the lift to the top, and he'd say, "There she is! Just starting down. The girl with the pink ski poles!" (That did make her easy to spot.)

All day long Ryan tried to time his runs so he could be in line the same time this girl was. He kept talking about her so much I finally said, "If you think she's so terrific, why don't you go introduce yourself?"

No way was he going to do that.

But we were on our way down the slope when I spotted the now familiar figure with the bright pink ski poles walking up the hill just below the big mogul jump. I stopped Ryan and pointed her out. "Now's your chance to impress her," I told him. "I'll go first and wait for you just below the jump. By the time she approaches that big mogul, you start down, hit the ramp, and really make an impression."

Ryan grinned and nodded. "Okay."

So I took off, hit the jump at a moderate speed, made a perfect landing, and skidded to a halt to wait for Ryan. There he was, rocketing down the slope. He'd timed it perfectly. The girl was going to be right there when he hit the jump. Ryan bent low and sped toward his takeoff point. The moment he hit the ramp, just a split second before he would go airborne, I shouted, "PINK POLES!"

Ryan completely lost it at that point. He went airborne all right. But instead of launching in a nice tight tuck, he went spread-eagled—which was pretty much how he landed as well. I started laughing, and I was still laughing when I got to where he was lying motionless—his face planted in the snow.

When he lifted his head, I was relieved to see Ryan was laughing too. "Great job!" I told him. "She definitely noticed you."

He threw a handful of snow at me, and I laughed again.

Despite that kind of luck with girls, Ryan and I managed to have fun in whatever we did. Ours was what I'd call a low-maintenance friendship. We didn't have to do anything special. We just enjoyed each other's company.

And we were good for each other. Because of his learning disability, Ryan worked incredibly hard to earn A's and B's in most of his classes. When he got home from school every afternoon, he went straight to his room and stayed there until he got all his homework and studying done. Through his example I learned a lot about discipline. And I think I had a good influence on him in terms of spontaneity and encouraging him to get out of his comfort zone and take risks.

Our personalities complemented each other. I was boisterous and outgoing; Ryan was shy and reserved. I was usually the idea person; Ryan was more of a follower. And yet Ryan was incredibly conscientious. He had a strong sense of right and wrong, and he carefully considered the consequences of every action. I can't count the number of times his hesitancy kept my impulsiveness from getting us both into trouble. I never had another friend like Ryan. And since he too was a Christian who shared the same spiritual interests, values, and commitment, we helped back up each other's spiritual beliefs. We were close enough to serve as each other's conscience, which is a great advantage in any friendship.

Ryan belonged to a different church, even a different denomination, down in Black Mountain. But he often did stuff with my youth group, and I did stuff with his.

However, I don't recall if he was with me when my home church, Montreat Presbyterian, celebrated "Youth Sunday" in April 1994. That was the day the members of the youth group took complete responsibility for morning worship—music, announcements, prayer, offering, and the sermon. So that spring of my sophomore year of high school I volunteered to speak, and I and an older girl in the youth group were selected to share the sermon time.

As I waited my turn to speak, I was surprised at how nervous the other kids acted. They used note cards, but still, from time to time, people stopped, stammered, and seemed to lose their place. All in all, they did fine. But their nervousness was obvious to me.

Watching my friends, I remembered my humiliation over *The Maury Povich Show*, and I told myself, *I'm not going to embarrass myself again by acting nervous! I WILL NOT!* I even prayed and asked God to help me stay calm. Some people might have felt a little extra pressure just because Dr. Billy Graham and his wife, Ruth, were in attendance that morning. But they were a regular part of our congregation whenever they were in town, so I didn't take any particular notice of them that day. In fact, when it was my turn, I actually felt relaxed as I stepped to the pulpit to deliver a three-point sermon I titled "The Ultimate Friend—The Ultimate Friendship."

I began by saying, "The ultimate friendship with the ultimate friend has a great COST." And I went on to refer to the accident, which most of the congregation already knew about:

I was rushed by ambulance from New Hampshire to Boston, where I was admitted to Boston Children's Hospital and given a 10 percent chance of survival. . . . After a few days my parents were told that I would have a greater chance of survival if I could be transferred across town to the Shriners Burn Institute, where they specialized in such severe cases involving children.

But there was a problem. There were only four beds in the whole Shriners Hospital for kids as badly burned as I was—and they were full! Everyone kept praying, and after several more days went by, there was an opening, and I began the long treatment of skin grafts and surgeries that, along with the Lord's intervention, saved my life.

After several weeks my parents found out how a bed had opened up for me. A young boy, burned over 90 percent of his body, fought for his life for four months, and then tragically he died. In order for me to enter the research hospital where my life was saved, a boy died. So I feel I have had a double blessing. A boy died so I could live here on earth. Jesus died so that I could live forever with him. Ultimate friendship with our ultimate friend has a great cost.

I then talked about our ultimate friendship having a second "C"—a COMMANDER. How Jesus said in John 15:14, "You are my friends if you do what I command." About how privileged we are to have a friendship with the King of the universe. Our ultimate friend is also the ultimate commander.

I concluded by saying that "our ultimate friendship has a cost, a commander, and a very select group of people CHOSEN to be part of this special relationship—

US. And Jesus has a very special purpose as stated in John 15:16, where he said he 'appointed you to go and bear fruit—fruit that will last!' ... The cost, the commander, and the chosen few are all elements of the ultimate friendship. The ultimate friend—the ultimate friendship. What a friend we have in Jesus!"

Once again I received very positive feedback from one of my speaking experiences. People lined up to compliment me after the service. Ironically, the only response that bothered me was the pastor's, who patted me on the back and announced, "I think you've heard the Call, Joel!"

I knew he was referring to God's "call" to become a preacher. And that annoyed me. I knew the pastor was trying to be affirming, but it felt to me like another case of someone looking at me and trying to put me in a box. I remember bristling and thinking, *Don't I get a choice in this?*

A day or two later I received another response, which I took a little better. Ruth Graham had taken the time to handwrite a note delivered to our house. It read as follows:

Dear Joel,

My heartfelt thanks for your warm, clear presentation of The Gospel! I have never heard it explained more simply, and it made me unspeakably grateful all over again that Someone died to make room for me. I will never forget it. God's hand is on your shoulder. Whatever lies ahead, you will be a true follower . . . able to communicate with people. And have fun at the same time.

Warmly,
Your friend, Ruth Graham

As much as I appreciated the encouragement from Mrs. Graham, I think her thoughtful note meant even more to my folks. They tucked it away someplace to keep for posterity.

The combination of that spiritual high (speaking in church for the first time) and the spiritual low point I had experienced after the breakup with my first real girlfriend helped me consider my faith in a whole new, and more serious, way. Actually, the contrast I'd seen between my values and those of my girlfriend while we were dating had made me step back and think. My youth group involvement, and especially the opportunities I'd had to serve on our mission projects, also played a major role. I'd considered myself a Christian since I'd asked Jesus to come into my life as we drove to the hospital that time when I was only four or five years old. But I'd reached a point of maturity in my life where I was beginning to realize the implications of a serious Christian commitment.

So when my sister Jami came home that summer after her first year of college to announce that she wanted to be baptized, my response was, "So do I!"

It might seem a little strange that we had grown up in a Christian family and gone to church all our lives, yet we'd never been baptized. However, we'd attended a Baptist church early in our lives—before we were old enough to go through the formal membership and baptism process. By the time we moved and started attending the Presbyterian church in Montreat, many of the kids our ages had already been baptized. So there hadn't been a set time for baptism, or a baptismal process everyone went through when they came of age.

There were plenty of other things going on at the time, so I just didn't think much about it. When I did think about it, I wasn't all that interested in being symbolically sprinkled—the way the sacrament is performed in most Presbyterian churches. I wanted a full-immersion baptism, and I was willing to wait until the time and opportunity presented itself.

My parents figured when we got old enough to understand the significance of the baptism ritual, we'd go through the experience. And that's just what happened.

Mom and Dad talked with the pastor emeritus of our church, Dr. Calvin Thielman, who said he'd be glad to baptize both Jami and me by immersion. And he had the perfect place in mind.

The Thielmans lived just a couple blocks away from us, in the bottom of the valley, with Flat Creek flowing right through their backyard. I'd grown up playing and hiking along and through that beautiful mountain stream. There was actually a small waterfall right behind the Thielmans' house, where the clear, cold water cascaded through rapids and spilled over a rocky ledge into a beautiful little pool, plenty wide and deep enough to serve as a baptismal font.

When I heard the plan, I was thrilled because I couldn't imagine a more beautiful or meaningful place. My folks went all out in preparation—inviting tons of friends and relatives to join us for food and the baptism service on the afternoon of August 18, 1994. We all planned and even printed out an order of service.

After the meal we began the service with a prayer and praise time. First we sang "Father, I Adore You" and then "As the Deer," the words of which seemed especially appropriate in that setting with the sound of running water echoing off the rocky walls of the valley:

> *As the deer panteth for the water,*
> *so my soul longeth after Thee.*
> *You alone are my heart's desire*
> *and I long to worship Thee.*
>
> *You alone are my Strength, my Shield,*
> *To You alone may my spirit yield.*
> *You alone are my heart's desire,*
> *And I long to worship Thee.*
>
> *You're my friend and You are my brother*
> *even though You are a King.*
> *I love You more than any other,*
> *so much more than anything.*
>
> *You alone are my Strength, my Shield,*
> *To You alone may my spirit yield.*
> *You alone are my heart's desire,*
> *And I long to worship Thee.**

We also sang the old traditional hymn "How Firm a Foundation" and listened to Scripture readings. Then Jami and I shared our own spiritual testimonies and recited the Apostles' Creed, and then it was time for the baptism itself.

Dr. Thielman stood in the middle of the pool, wearing a pair of insulated, chest-high, fishing waders. He told me later he just couldn't believe that it was such a perfect day when only a week before the volunteer firefighters had knocked on the door of his house to evacuate him and his wife due to the rising floodwaters of this creek in which we were about to be baptized. Even the day before he hadn't been sure the water level would have come down enough to have the service. But it was—if just barely. What was usually a fairly tranquil little stream roared and splashed and sprayed a lot more water than usual as it rushed around the normally calm pool that had formed behind several boulders.

I realized that my khakis and white dress shirt were not going to protect me from what I knew from experience was ice-cold water. But I wasn't even conscious of the temperature as I waded out into the stream. I was too excited and too wrapped up in the meaning of what I was doing to think of anything else. My heart and mind were too focused. I was about to take part in an almost 2,000-year-old ritual, making a public confession of my personal faith. I was letting the world know that it was my desire to follow Christ and live the rest of my life in obedience to him and to his Word.

As my pastor prepared to lower me back into the water, I remember a strange question popping into my mind: *Should I close my eyes or keep them open when I go under the water?* Surrounded by spraying mist, I heard Dr. Thielman say, "Joel Michael Sonnenberg, child of the covenant, I baptize you in the name of the Father, the Son, and the Holy Ghost." It was at that moment I made up my mind: since I can't close my eyes completely anyway, I'd keep them wide open so I wouldn't miss a single detail of what turned out to be one of the most memorable and meaningful experiences of my life.

In the days to come, I couldn't help but reflect on the unusual symbolism in the sights and sounds that day. The powerful currents rushing about me reminded me of my present need for God's peace in my life. The lapping of the water currents about me reminded me of the cleansing power of God's presence. And the mist that engulfed Jami and me as we were lowered into the water seemed to unite us in another profound life event we were privileged to share. We'd survived the fire. Now Jami and I were baptized with water together, signifying our dedication as disciples of Jesus Christ.

Words can't adequately express the feelings I had as I came up out of the water and into the light. But if I had to choose three, this is what I would say: alive; renewed; cleansed.

I felt ready for a new beginning.

Chapter 16

At first glance, this deeper commitment to following Jesus may have seemed to contradict my intention of testing and developing my leadership gifts. But the truth is, my desire to be a follower of Christ gave focus and purpose to my leadership ambitions.

My youth minister, Shawn Stewart, had a concept of leadership that I embraced, even before I fully understood it. He said leaders don't always have to stand in the front and have everyone else line up behind you. It's also possible to "lead from the center." To stand in the crowd, to participate in an event at the center of your peers—and from there to lead by example. Perhaps I could even use positive peer pressure to lead others to Christ by my example. I'd stuck out all my life; now I wanted to stick out with a purpose.

In emphasizing Jesus as our ultimate example, Shawn spent a lot of time and energy teaching about and letting us practice a style, a principle, a philosophy that Jesus embodied—servant leadership. Just as you can lead by example from the middle, you can also lead other people, not just by directing them, but by serving them. We practiced the concept on our summer mission trips, but Shawn also challenged us to put servant leadership into practice in our daily lives as well.

My sister Jami also had a great influence on my leadership goals and experiences during my high school years. When I was still in junior high and she was running for some student government office in high school, I remember helping her with campaign signs and talking while we worked together. I told her, "When I get to high school, I think I'll probably run for class president every year."

Jami told me that might not be a good idea.

"What do you mean?"

"You definitely don't want to be senior class president. Then you're stuck with planning class reunions the rest of your life." She said it would be smart to ease into student government. As a freshman, maybe run for an office few people want—like class treasurer—so you can become involved and learn the ropes. Then use that experience to run for class president in your sophomore year. Move up from class leadership to student body officer—maybe treasurer again—as a junior. Then run for student body president as a senior.

This was all just a casual conversation while sitting in my sister's room when I was an eighth grader. But I never forgot it. Jami made such good sense that when I reached high school, I followed her advice to a tee: class treasurer my freshman year. President of my sophomore class. A place on the student government cabinet as treasurer my junior year, with plans to run for president the next year.

Those formal leadership positions in student government earned me other leadership awards and opportunities. After my sophomore year I was selected as Owen High's HOBY ambassador—the school's lone representative to our state's Hugh O'Brian Youth Leadership conference in Charlotte, North Carolina. I also attended a Fellowship of Christian Athletes leadership conference. So I had my share of "upfront" leadership opportunities. But there were far more opportunities to "lead from the center" by getting involved and trying to be a positive example in everything I did—because I got involved in almost everything during high school.

In addition to student government duties, I was trained and took part in our school's "Peer Helper" program and was active in Owen High's chapter of Students Against Drunk Driving (SADD). I raised money for a student exchange program that brought children from war-torn sections of Ireland to visit and study in the United States. For a Christmas food-a-thon I collected the most groceries, which our school's vocational club then donated to a local Christian ministry that benefited the poor in our community. I volunteered to work with Special Olympics. One time I even agreed to be the chapel speaker at Montreat College.

And always there were sports. Soccer was my first love. I was quicker than I was fast. But despite my innate competitive instincts and considerable skill developed over the years, much of my success in soccer resulted as much from my attitude as it did from my athletic ability. Soccer presented more of a physical challenge for me than I usually let on.

Looking back, I can see why my parents worried about me playing soccer. With very little tissue over muscle and bone, I could get cuts easily. Since the top of my skull had been burned more than halfway through, Dad always wanted me to wear a helmet to protect my head and to keep my paper-thin, scar-tissue scalp from tearing open whenever I headed the ball. When I resisted because I didn't want to be the only one wearing a helmet, he lobbied the league to require helmets for everyone. But the idea never caught on. I did agree to wear a baseball cap for an added layer of protection.

But the susceptibility to wounds wasn't my greatest physical concern. The lack of sweat glands over most of my body was a much bigger problem in a long, strenuous game like soccer. Overheating was a constant danger. So during the flow of the game I had to find times I could run to the sideline and have someone throw water on me to cool me off.

Another problem was the inflexibility of my ankles. Because they wouldn't bend normally, I always had to run on the balls of my feet and on my toes—which usually made for the painful shin splints I had to learn to put up with if I wanted to play.

There were also some advantages to my disabilities. For example, whenever the referee called me for a "hand ball," I had a legitimate reason to complain. And I discovered that, early in a game, many first-time opponents were reluctant to mix it up with me—like they were afraid of somehow adding to my injuries. So I found that by taking it to my man at the beginning of any game, I had a distinct advantage until my opponent realized I wasn't going to break—and what's more, I was going to burn him bad if he didn't decide to step up and play good, hard soccer.

I played soccer well enough the fall of my junior year that I was named to the all-conference team as a midfielder. Another example of "leading from the middle"—literally.

Even in my role as manager of the varsity basketball team—a job usually thought to require more service than leadership—I looked for ways to make a difference, to change things for the better. Ryan volunteered to work as the team's scorekeeper, so the two of us went to the games and rode the bus together with the team. Together we decided to put a little more life and enthusiasm into the pregame festivities. So we jazzed things up by making a tape of a selection of lively and appropriate popular songs and playing it over the gymnasium's sound system during our team's warm-up drills. Our players and fans loved it.

Despite all these extracurricular activities, I usually held my own in the classroom. I'd never been a straight-A student. But in junior high and the first couple years of high school, I'd made mostly A's and B's without ever knocking myself out studying. All the way through school, mathematics had always been one of my strengths. I even tutored other students who had problems with math. However, that fall of my junior year I had my own problems with an Algebra II course.

I was barely keeping up when I had to miss two weeks for an operation on my arm and shoulder, which my doctors said would improve my range of motion. But because Owen High was on a block schedule in which each class met for two hours each day, missing two weeks of classes meant I was going to fall behind by four weeks. When I returned to school, I managed to muddle through and pass Algebra II. But when I began a precalculus course second semester, I was hopelessly lost. The teacher tried to help. My folks got me a tutor. I did extra assignments. I fought for weeks to catch up. But no matter what I tried, I fell farther and farther behind the rest of the class.

Until I finally decided, *I'll make what I make. I don't need this class to graduate.* And I threw in the towel. I quit trying.

I know this was just one class. But for me it felt like a major life turning point. I couldn't remember ever having given up on anything in my life. I'd been born with a big stubborn streak. My persistence not only played a huge role in my survival after the accident; it also enabled me to recover my health and learn to cope with my disabilities. I had never, never, never been a quitter. A big part of what other people always said they admired about me was my tenacity. I viewed determination as one of my greatest character traits—a major factor in my personal pride, confidence, and self-image.

Giving up, because it seemed so foreign, so unnatural, raised some serious questions in my mind.

So giving up, because it seemed so foreign, so unnatural, raised some serious questions in my mind. Maybe I wasn't such a determined person after all; maybe I had just deceived myself into thinking I was. Of course, once I started thinking that way, I began having all sorts of self-doubts. Did I really know myself at all? If I was a quitter, was I really qualified to be considered a leader? I obviously wasn't cut out to be a leader academically. I was going to have to find other ways to make a difference in my world.

I was still so anxious to make an impact, to be as much a leader as possible, that once basketball season ended, I volunteered to be manager of Owen High School's girls soccer team that spring.

At first I think Ryan and some of my other buddies questioned my sanity for signing up to hang around school an extra couple of hours every day, toting water and dragging big bags of soccer balls around the field. But it wasn't long before they began to realize, *Ya know, Joel gets to spend a couple hours every day watching some pretty good-looking girls run up and down the soccer field. And then there's those rides to away games when he's the only guy on the bus. Hey, Sonnenberg's no dummy!*

My creative approach to girls was further demonstrated by a plan I figured almost guaranteed me a great time at the prom my junior year.

I decided to ask one of my sister Jami's college friends. Long before this girl and Jami went to Taylor University together, her family had been friends of our family for years at CAMP-of-the-WOODS in New York. Her father had played quarterback when my dad was a lineman on Taylor University's football team back in the 1960s. I'd known Jordan, and she'd known me, for much of our lives. I thought she would make *the* perfect prom date. We were already friends. There would be no "romantic" awkwardness. I could relax and just have fun at my junior prom.

There were, of course, a couple other minor considerations. Like the prestige I would gain by showing up at my high school prom with a college woman on my arm. And the fact that I thought Jordan Jerele Berner was perhaps the single most gorgeous girl I'd ever known.

Oh, yeah, one other thing: I was almost certain if I asked Jordan to go to the prom with me, she would say yes.

I ran my plan by my parents and my sister Jami. Everyone liked it. So I called to ask Jordan if she would be my prom date. She said she would.

I could hardly wait.

The night promised to be even more special than I imagined when I learned I was in the running for "Prince of the Prom." The tradition at Owen High was to elect a queen and king for homecoming every fall, and then a princess and prince for the spring prom.

I was honored just to be named as one of the members of the Shawana Court, but for some reason I was absent on the day our class voted for prince and princess. I thought it a little odd the next day when my homeroom teacher insisted I fill out a prom prince and princess ballot. Stranger still was her "casual" remark about me not needing to feel it would be improper to vote for myself. I checked the name of one of my classmates instead. And then I didn't think about it again, as I finalized plans for what I expected to be a wonderfully memorable evening.

Jami flew home with Jordan the weekend of the prom. As my sister and my mother spent much of that Saturday helping get my date ready for the prom, I began to realize an unanticipated advantage to my plan. I was only going to have to deal with one mother's expectations. And my mom's concerns were more focused on getting Jordan ready than they were on me. Which didn't make me feel slighted in the least.

Departure time finally arrived. There were oohs and aahs all around the Sonnenberg living room. Cameras flashed before we could make our exit. I eventually escorted my date out to the sleek, maroon Jaguar a friend had loaned me to drive for the evening. At the end of the street I stopped the car, and Jordan and I prayed and asked God to bless the entire evening.

After a relaxed dinner at a classy restaurant with a bunch of my friends, Jordan and I got back in the Jag and headed for the elegant Biltmore Estate. At one time the palatial North Carolina residence of the Vanderbilt family, the Biltmore Estate is now one of Asheville's most renowned tourist attractions, and on this evening the magnificently luxurious setting for Owen High School's junior-senior prom.

We arrived at the Biltmore fashionably late. Most of my classmates were already inside. Entering the ballroom—Jordan looking appropriately regal in her stunning gown, me jauntily twirling my cane and trying to look distinguished in my top hat and tails—we paused momentarily to survey the opulent scene.

Our "entrance" into this storybook setting felt like something out of a classic old movie. For as we stood in the doorway, quickly appraising the milling, murmuring crowd, I heard someone announce, "Hey, look! There's Joel." Every head seemed to turn in unison, and every eye in the house focused on us. I couldn't have staged a better moment if I'd tried. I knew even then that I'd never forget it. The night could have ended right then, and all the effort would have been worth it.

Instead, I turned and grinned at Jordan. "Come on," I said. "I want to introduce you to my friends."

Before the night was over, I was crowned co-prince of the prom—sharing the honors with the guy I voted for. One more detail that fell into place to make for a truly magical, memorable evening.

But prom wasn't the last or only great memory I took from the last few months of my junior year.

My drafting instructor, Mr. Morgan, had already asked me to take part in an AutoCAD demonstration for a statewide technical conference. I'd enrolled in a drafting class, having had no idea how much physical dexterity was required to manipulate rulers, compasses, and a wide variety of other gadgets in order to produce mechanical drawings that were not only reproducible but accurate within a fraction of a millimeter. With only one hand and no fingers, the class would have been impossible for me had it not been for a very patient instructor—and a computer program that enabled me to use a mouse and a keyboard to digitally create on-screen the exact drawings my classmates produced at their drafting tables using paper and pencils. Because I'd proved so proficient with the program, I received the honor of demonstrating the possibilities to teachers from other schools around the state.

Not long after that, my principal, Mr. Randolph, told me he had a favor to ask of me. He and I had always had a great relationship, so I accepted his invitation to deliver a guest lecture to the students in a graduate course on "The Psychology of Special Children," which he was taking at the University of South Carolina. As a high school student I would have felt honored just by the opportunity to lecture to a classroom full of graduate students; but I was even more pleased to think that my high school principal trusted me enough to ask me to teach his grad school class. And that he respected me enough to believe I had something worth saying.

Another significant experience that spring came after one of the school guidance counselors suggested I apply for a special scholarship program called the "Tribute Award," sponsored by Discover Card in cooperation with the American Association of School Administrators. These tribute awards are unique in that they honor students who not only achieve in school but have demonstrated outstanding accomplishment in the community and in their personal lives.

I spent hours and hours doing the preliminary paperwork. My folks helped me think of and list all the organizations I'd been a part of, my work experience, every volunteer effort I'd been involved in, every award received in my lifetime, and most of the speaking opportunities, television appearances, and newspaper interviews I'd done to share my story. That took a while.

Then I had to collect letters of recommendation that addressed my character, my achievements, and my leadership abilities. But the primary requirement was writing a series of mini-essays about the obstacles I've overcome, my leadership experience, my community service, my special talents, and my future goals.

A few weeks after I completed and submitted the paperwork, I got a phone call notifying me that what I had written had won me the first-place Gold Award for the state of North Carolina in the Science, Business & Technology category of the 1995 Discover Card Tribute Award program. That meant I had won a $2,500 scholarship and would be in the running for a national award.

In mid-May I received written notification from Discover Card, congratulating me as the recipient of a national award. I was one of nine high school juniors whose essays had won a national Silver Tribute Award to be presented at a special awards ceremony in Chicago the following month.

At the end of June, Discover Card flew me and my parents to Chicago, put us up in the downtown Ritz-Carlton, showed us the sights for three days, and honored all nine winning essayists with a gala affair. The awards banquet itself featured football coach Lou Holtz as the emcee, professionally produced video tributes to each of the winners, and celebrity presenters such as figure-skating great Scott Hamilton and entertainer Trisha Yearwood, who handed us our awards. I had a blast, got to meet a bunch of interesting people, and received another $15,000 scholarship as part of the national award.

Many of the articles written about me winning the tribute award quoted from the essay I wrote, which began this way:

Have you ever walked into a room and all eyes were upon you? Imagine this: you are in front of a crowd of hundreds or even thousands of people. Suddenly everyone turns their heads and gasps at your appearance. This may be your dream; it is my living nightmare. Young children cry and run from me. Older kids have said, "Look at the monkey!" Adults have told me, "Take off your mask!" Others have left restaurants in disgust—stating I was ruining their meal.

At the age of twenty-two months I was severely burned in an automobile crash. Only a few inches remain on my body that look normal. The top of my head was burned so severely that my skull was exposed for several years. In the beginning the doctors gave me little chance of surviving, and if I did survive, they said I wouldn't be able to live a normal life. The car accident left me with an injury that the experts described as one of the worst they had ever seen. In addition to my skull injury, my nose, ears, eyelids, and lips were gone. My smooth skin, all my fingers and toes, and a hand were burned off. Now fifteen years later, I have had forty-five operations and have spent almost two years of my life in the hospital. Still I live life with facial and bodily disfigurement.

When your beauty is gone, what do you do? Consciously and unconsciously, I emphasized my personality over my appearance. When almost everything I did was an obstacle to overcome, I developed what I could do and tried to forget what I couldn't do. Despite deep burns completely around my legs, I learned to not only walk but run. From my earliest years in preschool, I have played soccer, and I am good at it (varsity all-conference honors this past season as a junior).

Learning to ride a bike was tough, but I did it. I learned to hold on without fingers. I now enjoy mountain biking. Learning to swim seemed impossible. But I learned to swim and dive and now enjoy scuba diving, snorkeling, knee boarding (behind a speedboat), and boogie boarding (in the surf). . . . I am a competitor. . . .

To overcome the barrier of my disfigurement, I've learned to help others feel more comfortable around me. I often try to create fun with a sense of humor that puts others at ease. I have also learned to laugh even at myself and my condition. And I have deliberately developed skills in games such as Ping-Pong, pool, and foosball in order to bridge to others.

My faith in God and my belief that He has saved me for His purpose is my light in what could often seem a dark world. The promise that He is always with me, that He doesn't see outwardly but looks on the heart of all people, is the reason I have been able to overcome extreme physical and mental barriers in my own body, geographical changes, and societal rejection.

Some people work their whole lives to be able to walk into a room and be recognized by large numbers of people. I already have this ability because I survived a life-threatening injury as a child. Now we just have to work on the applause!

I came home from Illinois feeling flattered and grateful for the national recognition I'd received and excited about my coming senior year. I now firmly believed one of the other things I'd written in my tribute award essay: "I was saved to be a leader."

But as I looked forward to my final year of high school and my last year of living at home, I couldn't help thinking, *There can be no way for it to measure up to this past year.*

I was wrong.

Chapter 17

One of the highlights came even before the following school year began. I planned, organized, and led a summer mission team made up of youth from Montreat Presbyterian Church and a group from a sister church in Harlem, New York. Our team repaired the homes and cleaned up the property of two elderly women in the Black Mountain area. My supervision and involvement in the effort served as my Eagle project, the last requirement for scouting's highest rank.

Then the school year started, and my senior year soon proved to be the busiest year of my life. Following the advice Jami had given me four years earlier, I ran for student body president, which meant I would play a visible role in many school activities. Not only did I preside over both executive and student council meetings, but I also was on the platform with the administrators and guests every time we had an assembly program in the auditorium. Routinely, I was by the microphone down on the floor during pep rallies in the gymnasium.

Then there were the daily trips to the principal's office, where I'd sit on one side of the desk and Mr. Randolph would sit on the other and hand me the PA microphone as he said, "Now with today's announcements, here's Mr. Sonnenberg."

One day early in the year, when Mr. Randolph wasn't in his office, I took the initiative to make the end-of-day announcements on my own. When I finished, I went ahead and dismissed school without realizing it was fifteen minutes before the end of the school day.

My fellow students didn't seem to mind. In fact, they practically sprinted out of the building, hoping to reach their cars before someone called them back. The surprised reaction of the administrative staff clued me in to my mistake even before a very alarmed Mr. Randolph rushed into the office. "What are you doing dismissing school?" he demanded to know. "The buses aren't even here yet!"

Oops! I tried very hard not to laugh, as I truthfully explained that it had all been an honest mistake.

Mr. Randolph may have had some doubts about my innocence to begin with, but I think I eventually convinced him that I hadn't realized what time it was. "Okay," he finally conceded, looking me right in the eye, "but it better not happen again."

I had a great relationship with Mr. Randolph. The next day he was laughing about the whole thing. Still, I made sure never to dismiss school early again.

Not that I couldn't have used a little extra time most days. While still enrolled at Owen High, I also signed up for a couple courses at Montreat College that year. The classes I took in English Comp and Downhill Skiing counted as language and PE credits toward my high school diploma and would transfer with me so I could start college the following year with a few college credit hours already earned.

Outside of class, soccer took up time most afternoons. My teammates elected me cocaptain of the varsity squad my senior year, and I earned all-conference honors as the team's best midfielder. During the fall I went through my Eagle Scout ceremony, the culmination of all those years and all that I'd worked for in scouting. Also in November I was asked to address a plenary session of the Phoenix Society's World Burn Congress, held in St. Louis that year. I spoke on the conference theme—"Growing Beyond Survival."

I never did know for sure what triggered her interest again, though it may have been the news coverage of my Discover Card Tribute Award Scholarship back during the summer. But NBC's Chicago news anchor Carol Marin, the same reporter who'd included my story in her television special on facial disfigurement back when I was five years old and eight years old, asked permission to come to North Carolina to film a follow-up.

The two days she spent shadowing me in the halls of Owen High—shooting soccer footage, talking to teachers and friends, interviewing me and the rest of my family in our home in Montreat—made me feel good about Carol Marin

as a reporter. Some news coverage of my Discover Card scholarship had bugged
me. Headlines such as "Burn Victim Thrives on Challenges" and "Burned Teen
Succeeds Against the Odds," like so many stories over the years, seemed more
focused on what had happened to me sixteen years earlier than on who I was
today. I was portrayed as (1) a victim people should feel sorry for because of the
horrible thing that had happened to him, or (2) a victim everyone should admire,
in an almost godlike way, for overcoming the terrible tragedy that had "ruined"
his life. Both approaches played on pity by viewing me primarily as a victim—
either as a suffering victim or an overcoming one.

Carol Marin seemed to see beyond the clichés. Of course, she told what happened to me at that toll plaza in New Hampshire in 1979, but her interest always
went deeper than that. Instead of portraying me as someone "different" who is
either worse off than others or somehow better than everyone else because of
what I'd overcome, she wanted to go deeper. She was more interested in learning who I really was.

Carol didn't seem as interested in hearing the specifics of people's cruel
responses to me as she was in my honest feelings about the staring and the insensitive comments. I admitted to her, "When it happens, it pierces me. I just don't
show it."

She asked, "You never get used to it, do you?"

"Not yet!" I told her.

She asked other tough questions—such as, "What
about dating and girls?"

I told her, "It's not nearly as bad as some people probably think."

"Do you want to get married and have kids someday?" she asked.

"I hope so," I told her. "I pray . . ."

She also wanted to know, "Do you ever say to yourself, 'If God is such a merciful, kind God, how come he gives some people such difficulties to endure?'"

I told her, "God never gives us more than we can handle."

"You believe that?"

I assured her I did.

I've done enough interviews over the years to know you can't know for certain how any story is going to turn out until you see it in the paper or on the
screen. But when NBC sent me a copy of the two-part story that aired in Chicago

> *I told her, "God never gives us more than we can handle."*

that November, I was satisfied that Carol Marin had understood and tried to honestly portray who I was and what I'd wanted to say.

I felt the story was summed up by one of my assistant principals, who was quoted on camera as saying, "Joel is the most normal person I know. Perfect? I can't speak to that. But normal, yes!"

That made me feel good.

The public attention I received seemed to mushroom in the weeks and months that followed.

First I received word that I was in the running to be a torchbearer when the Olympic flame was to come through Western North Carolina the following summer on its way to the Summer Games in Atlanta. The local United Way had started a search to identify and select forty "community heroes" to do the honors. I'd been nominated and would find out after the first of the year if I'd been chosen.

Shortly after learning about the torch possibility, I found out I'd also been nominated for the honor of the *Asheville Citizen-Times* 1995 Citizen of the Year, an annual poll the newspaper conducts among its readers. The next thing I knew, I was informed that I had been selected by the newspaper as one of the finalists. In mid-December the *Citizen-Times* began running the ballot—which meant that my picture, along with the photos of ten other finalists, appeared in the paper every day in a box under the headline:

**Vote for Your Hero
for the 1995
Citizen of the Year**

The paper also ran a long, two-part, front-page feature story, complete with photos of me with my little brother, Kyle; with my family; interacting with friends at school; playing soccer; and so on. Part 1, titled "So Much Taken," introduced me this way:

Seeing Joel Sonnenberg for the first time isn't easy.

Many turn their heads. Others gasp and walk away. Children may cry and cling to their mothers.

But mostly people stare. They stare until they can process the sight in their minds, make sense of what's before them.

> Joel knows it's hard. Instead of living his life preparing for the world, he's spent his years preparing a world for him . . .

Most of the article told about the accident and the aftermath, spelling out the physical and factual details of my life journey. But it also gave a fairly flattering picture of my life today:

> Here, among high school beauties and heartthrobs, Joel is a standout, without question the school's leader. A hero. He is student body president, soccer team co-captain, rushing across the hard ground with no toes, his shins and ankles aching from the movement forced beneath thick, unyielding scars.
>
> He played drums in the band, despite a missing left hand and no fingers on the other. But he kept trying and was named "Most Improved Drummer" by the bandleader.
>
> Every day he kept believing, telling himself he could do anything he wanted, anything other kids could do . . .

Part 2 of the feature, titled "So Much to Give," ran the following day and went a little deeper to talk about my current high school experience and my plans for the future. It probably overemphasized my achievements by talking about all the things I was involved in. But it made it clear I hadn't done it all on my own:

> "My parents' outlook was that I was going to have to prove I can do it," [Joel] said. "Everything that I've accomplished is way beyond their wildest dreams. They were just hoping I was going to live."
>
> Joel gives them all the credit, saying if they hadn't pushed, he wouldn't have had the will to continue.
>
> But the true test of all this teaching, the pushing, has yet to come. In the fall, Joel will enter Taylor University, a private college in Indiana where his older sister, Jami, is a junior.
>
> For the first time in his life, he will be on his own, away from a family who protected and prepared him, away from the friends who got beyond the scars.
>
> He will start over. And it won't be easy: the explaining, the preparation, the amounts of energy he must invest to win others over.
>
> "I'm ready," he says. "I want to see how I do on my own. My parents have always been there to shield me. It's time to move on."

Joel has found a metaphor to illustrate his feelings about leaving home. "It's like a trapeze," he says. "You have to let go of one rope to get on the next."

Whatever rope he grabs, those who are watching will call him a miracle.

It is a miracle Joel Sonnenberg is alive.

But more than that is a bigger miracle. That a child with so much taken would become a man with so much to give.*

All in all, I felt they were nice, balanced articles that didn't just play for sympathy. How much they influenced the Citizen of the Year voting, I have no idea. For a time I wasn't sure anyone even noticed the ballots in the paper. But then I was in the school office one day when Mrs. Johnson, one of the assistant principals, told me she hoped I won. "I voted for you five times already," she said.

"No kidding? Thanks!" It really did make me feel honored. I hadn't imagined that someone like that would actually be calling in and voting for me. Evidently lots of people did. I was soon informed that at a special banquet the first Saturday of the new year I would be recognized as *Asheville Citizen-Times* 1995 Citizen of the Year for Western North Carolina. I couldn't believe it. I was even more excited a few weeks later to learn that I was also one of the forty "community heroes" who would be honored to carry the Olympic torch that coming summer. Once again there was an article and picture in the paper.

There was more publicity in other parts of the country that winter and spring as well. When I was asked to speak as part of a special lecture series at Georgetown (Kentucky) College, the Lexington media covered my visit. And then there was the opportunity to speak to the entire student body in a chapel service at Taylor University in Upland, Indiana—where Jami was a student and where I planned to enroll the following school year.

———

*Susan Reinhardt, "So Much Taken ... So Much to Give," *Asheville Citizen-Times*, December 17–18, 1995. Copyright © 2004, *Asheville, N.C.*, *Citizen-Times*. Reprinted with permission.

Despite all these things happening outside of school, I determined to make the most of my senior year at Owen High. My term as student body president was made all the more special because my buddy Ryan served as my vice president, and Barrett McFatter, who'd been a great friend of ours since third grade, was treasurer. Student government wasn't something Ryan would have ever easily considered on his own. The thought of having to stand up in front of an audience and make a speech terrified him. I promised that I'd run the meetings and handle the up-front stuff. I assured him that, if he'd step out of his shell and just back me up, we'd have a great time running the student government together.

Like me, Ryan ran unopposed. So we were in.

The school gave us one entire free class period each day to devote to student government business. That was more than enough time to hold "official" cabinet meetings with the secretary and treasurer. These were actually more like laid-back brainstorming sessions in which we planned student government events, carried out assorted official duties, and generally had a terrific time. We pretty much had the run of the school.

I'd noticed during my time in high school that student government, especially council meetings, didn't inspire a lot of participation or respect. Most of what was done seemed unimaginative. Dull even. So one of my goals was to liven and loosen things up.

Why, I got to thinking, *did all student government meetings have to be held in the library? What could be duller than that?* So we sometimes held meetings outdoors. We actually held a student council sleepover at the school one time. Anything to increase school spirit and make student council fun and different. I even spiced up the daily announcements with a joke or thought for the day—dumb stuff like, "Do vegetarians eat animal crackers? If so, do they eat them head first?"

We started a number of traditions that continue today. Before the big annual football game with our archrival, Reynolds High, we bought an old car from a local junkyard, painted it Reynolds' school color, and called it "The Green Machine." We raised money for student government by charging Owen High students a dollar per whack to smash the car with a sledgehammer.

We were discussing ideas to add prestige or perks to student government so more people would be interested when we hit on another idea that has lasted. Parking spots in the student lot at Owen High were always at a premium. Some people arrived at school twenty to thirty minutes early every morning, especially in bad weather, just to claim the prime places nearest the school. So to entice more students to consider joining student government in the future, we petitioned and got approval from the school to reserve the choice parking spots for student government leaders—starting the following year.

The best enticement would have been for Ryan and me to tell people what an absolute blast we were having. But we didn't want to spoil a good thing.

When I said we had the run of the school, I meant that literally. If we didn't have pressing business to do, we'd use our student government period to go to the gym and shoot baskets, or we'd go sit in the teachers' lounge for a coffee break and shoot the breeze with our favorite instructors. Ryan and I were on a first-name basis with the janitorial staff. And the lunchroom ladies loved us too.

Our student government period fell right in the middle of the day, so we'd often go to the cafeteria between the staggered lunch hours. That way Ryan and I could go through the line when no one else was there, cut up with the ladies who served us, and have the entire cafeteria to ourselves. One day toward the end of school, we went into the cafeteria kitchen early in the morning and asked the cooks if they would prepare a special meal just for the two of us. They laughed and asked what we wanted. We requested one of our favorites—ravioli.

They checked and told us they had just one container left on the shelves. "But if you boys come in between lunch periods today when no one else is here, you can have your ravioli."

I have no idea what the rest of the school ate that day. Maybe mystery meat. But we felt like royalty, with our own exclusive menu. And we got to go back for seconds!

When we had free time, Ryan and I often volunteered to help out in the office. The secretaries could almost always find something for us to do. We especially enjoyed sorting and putting mail in the teachers' boxes. On more than one occasion we collected all the junk mail for the entire school and crammed it into the mailbox of Mr. Morgan, our favorite industrial arts teacher. Then we hung around to watch his reaction when he came to pick up his mail.

The principal, Mr. Randolph, was also the butt of more than a few practical jokes. We circled his car with traffic cones one day so he couldn't back out of his parking spot without having to collect them all. Another time we parked a car behind his so he couldn't leave until we went out and moved the vehicle.

Then there was the time he left the building and we covered his entire office with—I don't remember how many—cans of Silly String. By the time we finished, the place looked like Spiderman had gone insane in there. We couldn't exactly hang around and wait to see the reaction to that prank. But then it didn't take long to find out what happened. No sooner did Mr. Randolph return and open the door to his office than the school intercom came on and I heard a very stern voice saying, "Joel Sonnenberg, please report to the office!"

I don't know why he thought of me. Fortunately, he was laughing when he said, "Very funny, Joel! Now get every bit of that stuff out of here!" I'd anticipated his response, which is why we'd used Silly String. It makes a great visual impression, yet it isn't terribly difficult to clean up.

Chapter 18

When Ryan and I went to a movie together just a couple of weeks before our senior prom, we joked about filming an appeal for dates and paying the theater's advertising rates to include the clip among the ad spots they ran with the previews. The truth was, we didn't have any idea who we were going to ask to the last prom of our high school careers. And it was only a couple weeks away.

Thankfully, there was a student government conference at nearby North Buncombe High School in Asheville the very next week. Student leaders from a number of area schools were invited to attend and to share ideas. One of the North Buncombe students hosting the conference just happened to be Allison Randolph, the daughter of my principal. We'd met before, so we hung out and talked some during the conference.

Allison was not only friendly and smart; she was very cute. I toyed with the idea of asking her that day but decided I didn't know her that well, and I wasn't sure how she'd feel about being asked to the prom at the school where her dad served as principal. But I was encouraged the day after the conference when I returned to Owen High School and Mr. Randolph made a special point to say, "You were the subject of some interesting conversation during supper at my house last night, Joel." The way he smiled as he said it made me hope that maybe Allison had found me as interesting as I found her.

I called and asked. She said yes. And I had my date for the prom a whole week ahead. And Ryan had met a friend of Allison's at the conference. So I acted as a go-between to encourage him to ask her. When she said yes, our plans were set.

Almost.

I'd had such a memorable time the year before that I wanted my senior prom to be just as special. I already had a plan, and I decided I needed help executing only one part.

Admittedly, the Jaguar I drove to the prom the year before set an imposing precedent. So this year I told my father, "I want to go to this prom in the sweetest convertible possible. It doesn't have to be new or snazzy. Just a classy convertible." That was the one thing I had my heart set on.

I laughed when Dad rolled his eyes. We both knew it wasn't going to be easy. "I'll see what I can find," he told me.

"That's the spirit, Dad!" I cheered.

And he started making phone calls to friends and car dealers to locate something I could borrow or rent for the evening. I think he called practically everyone we knew and nearly every car dealer listed in the Yellow Pages without any luck. Finally he talked to the sales manager of the nearby Fletcher BMW dealer. The fellow didn't seem too hopeful to begin with, but Dad really poured it on, explaining that this was the one request I'd made of him for my senior prom. I guess he told the guy a little about me—that I'd been named Citizen of the Year and was scheduled to be a torchbearer for the Olympic flame that summer. That seemed to pique his interest, perhaps because BMW was one of the official sponsors of the Olympic Torch Relay, or maybe he hoped there might be some free publicity in the thing. "Okay," he told my father. "I think I can help you."

"A convertible?" my dad wanted to know. "Joel says it has to be a convertible."

"We can do that. What was the date again?"

Dad told him, and he said to stop by early the afternoon of the prom and he'd have a car ready.

The big day finally arrived, and I rolled out of bed incredibly early to launch my plan to make this a memorable occasion for Allison, as well as for me. I'd cleared the plan with Mr. Randolph, so he and his wife were waiting for me when I drove up to their house at seven o'clock that Saturday morning. They escorted me into their formal dining room, where I laid out two place settings of my mother's best china, silverware, cloth napkins, and crystal. I gave a bouquet of flowers to Mrs. Randolph.

After I unpacked the rest of my supplies in the kitchen, I set to work fixing Allison a very special breakfast. And when I had it almost ready, Mr. and Mrs. Randolph called a very surprised and groggy Allison down to the dining room, where I presented her with a single long-stemmed rose, seated her at the table, and then brought out the hot waffles topped with fresh strawberries and whipped cream. I think she was dazzled. Which was my intent. I wanted every part of the day to be special.

At the conclusion of a very enjoyable breakfast, I cleaned up in the kitchen, packed up all my culinary paraphernalia, and let Allison know what time I'd be back to pick her up that evening. Then after I returned home, Dad and I headed for our appointment at the BMW dealer in nearby Fletcher, North Carolina.

Neither one of us had any idea what kind of car would be waiting for me. "I told him what you wanted. He said he had a car," Dad assured me. "We'll just have to see."

I feared the worst. *It's gonna be the only rusty BMW convertible I've ever seen in my life.*

The sales manager was waiting when we got to his lot. My father introduced me. "This is my son Joel." We shook hands.

"I think I have something that should suit you just fine," the man smiled. "Follow me." He led us through the showroom and down some stairs to a lower level that was dark and shadowed. I took a large gulp. When he opened an outside door to let in some light, he turned and grinned at me. "This is your lucky day, Joel."

He motioned behind me with his hand. And when I turned around, I could not believe my eyes. There in front of me was a gorgeous, glistening, red, brand-new BMW Z–3—the exact same car featured in the latest James Bond movie. This was the first year BMW made this model. They were impossible to find— all over the country people were on waiting lists to buy one. These were some of the hottest wheels on the planet. *This is what I'm driving to my prom?!*

I looked at Dad. He was shaking his head and grinning. "No way! I don't believe it," he told me.

All I could say was "Awesome!"

"Here are the keys, Joel," the sales manager said. "Hope you have a great time this evening. You can bring the car back in the morning."

"THANKS!" I told him. "This is just fantastic!" I had never imagined . . .

I was literally shaking as I very carefully drove the car home from the dealership. Dad followed. And every time I looked in my rearview mirror I could see this huge, disbelieving grin on his face.

After I got dressed for the evening, and before I headed for Allison's house to pick her up, I called her father. "You might want to be watching when I drive up, Mr. Randolph," I said. But I didn't tell him why.

A few minutes later, when I pulled to a stop in front of his house, Mr. Randolph hurried out to greet me. "What do you think?" I grinned, as I climbed out of the car.

"Wow!"

Allison liked the car too—though I don't think she was quite as impressed as her father and my father were. I guess it's a guy thing.

We had a wonderfully memorable evening that began as we joined a dozen or so of my friends for a very classy dinner at an expensive restaurant. Ryan was there with Allison's friend. Allison knew some people from Owen High. When I introduced her to those she hadn't met, everyone seemed favorably impressed with the principal's daughter. I know I was. And not just because she looked spectacular.

After dinner we went to the Biltmore Estate for the actual prom. By the time the evening was over, we'd hit it off so well that I had decided I would ask her out again. And I was pretty sure she would be glad if I would.

I figured if I was going to keep dating my principal's daughter, I needed to have her home when I'd promised. So I did. But even though it was the wee hours of the morning by then, my evening was not quite finished. It was 4:30 a.m. when I got to Ryan's house. He hadn't gotten back from taking his date home, so while I waited for him, I took his mom for a spin in the BMW. Ryan pulled into the driveway about the same time his mom and I did, so I asked him, "Wanna go for a ride?"

"Sure thing!" he replied.

He jumped in, and we drove to the local grocery store, where I let him drive around the parking lot a few times before he delivered his verdict: "Sweet!" A few minutes later I dropped him off back at his house and headed home to get a few hours sleep before I reluctantly returned my ride to the dealer and rode home again in my father's pumpkin of a Honda.

Allison and I did date for a couple months. And we remained friends after that. But since we were heading off in different directions to different colleges in the fall, we mutually agreed not to pursue a dating relationship any farther.

Graduation came before I knew it. As student body president, I sat on stage in the Thomas Wolfe auditorium in Asheville along with various school administrators and visiting dignitaries. Decked out in my maroon cap and gown, with honor cords in different colors wrapped around my neck.

The commencement speaker was none other than bestselling crime novelist Patricia Cornwell, an alumnus of our school. Having learned it was her big fortieth birthday, I surprised her after my introduction by lighting a candle on a cupcake and leading the entire audience in singing "Happy Birthday." After the ceremony I went home with all my family and friends for a huge party, where we ate tons of food and enjoyed live music on our torch-lit porches.

As big a highlight for me as my high school commencement was the special graduation trip I took a week later with my father and my grandpa. I had my choice of destinations, but I knew Grandpa had always wanted to see Alaska. That sounded good to me too. So that's where we headed.

We spent one week exploring—traveling to Fairbanks by train, watching wildlife like bald eagles and moose in their natural habitat, seeing Mount McKinley, enjoying the wilderness. The rest of the time we spent fishing. Deep-sea fishing for halibut in the Gulf of Alaska. Then angling for salmon on inland rivers.

That fishing thrill of a lifetime was followed by a different kind of thrill just a couple weeks after we returned from Alaska with two coolers full of frozen fish to share with family and friends. The Olympic flame was winding its way across country, and the organizers for the western Carolina leg were finalizing all the details. As a torchbearer I received official how-to instructions on everything— how to dress, how to hold the torch, how to pass the flame, etc., etc.

My official Olympic torchbearer uniform came in the mail. I couldn't imagine wearing it, but with every passing day the flame was getting closer and closer. Then my torch came. Ohh, was it sweet! I pictured my own Olympic torch hanging up on my bedroom wall—how cool it would look. I also hefted the torch up a few times to make sure I could run with it and hold on okay. But I still hadn't heard where in the progression through our mountains my run would take place.

Finally a letter came in the mail, showing the torch run itself, with each leg of the run charted. "Joel," my mom announced, "I don't believe it! You have the first leg—after the torch makes it to City-County Plaza! Right there at the courthouse!" That meant I would be in the center of all the downtown activity. *What an honor to be chosen to run that first segment!*

There was even an official printout for every participant, with a minute-by-minute schedule that told me exactly when I should begin my one-kilometer (six-tenths of a mile) run and where and in what direction I should turn. Not one detail was left to chance. Organizers had everything timed down to the minute. It said so on my copy of the official schedule of the "1996 Olympic Torch Relay, Region 5: Day 61, Wed., June 26 / Greenville to Knoxville."

Even so, when the big day arrived, the flame was almost twenty minutes late arriving in the City-County Plaza in front of the courthouse in downtown Asheville for the ceremony and kickoff celebration with the mayor and members of the Atlanta Committee for the Olympic Games. But I didn't mind the wait. It gave me that much longer to survey the scene and begin to anticipate what was about to happen.

On one level I'd looked forward to this day for months. But with everything else that had gone on in my life, I think I viewed this as just one more honor in a long list of special opportunities granted me. The significance of it all didn't begin to sink in until I stood in that downtown square, waiting for the arrival of that ancient flame that had come all the way from Greece and was on its way to an Olympic ceremony in Atlanta that would be watched by a billion people around the world. This was more than just another individual honor. On this day I was just one small part of something larger—much larger—than myself.

Not only had I been selected from among millions of Americans to carry the torch on one leg of its journey, but the local committee had chosen me to be the one to light my torch from the cauldron during Asheville's official ceremony and run the flame on the first leg out of the plaza. As I stood at the edge of the platform, waiting for the arrival of the flame, I looked out over the thousands of excited spectators crowded into that downtown square and pictured my upcoming exit while carrying the flame. *This is going to be awesome!*

And it was.

I can't adequately describe my adrenaline rush as I strode up the steps of the stage at City-County Plaza. Then came the signal we had been waiting for—the flame itself appeared above the heads of the crowd. Rhythmic waves of sounds— clapping, shouting, and yelling—filled the air around us. The runner dipped his torch to light the giant cauldron in front of us. And with that the formalities began.

When the fifteen-minute ceremony ended, I lit my torch from the burning cauldron. As I lifted that centuries-old flame, thousands of highly animated faces oohed, aahed, and shouted their approval. At the crowd's roar I thrust the flame out above my chest as if beckoning others to grab it and run with me.

I then strode down the steps with my flaming torch held high, away from my face and eyes, as thousands clapped. I turned onto College Street and began running through the heart of Asheville.

As the roar of the plaza crowd faded behind me, the people lining the street ahead began to applaud and cheer in a rolling wave of acclaim that lifted, carried, and followed me every step of my run. I felt like a conquering hero hailed by grateful legions as I ran past that continuous line of strangers regularly laced with the familiar faces of Montreat neighbors, teachers, schoolmates, friends, and family. As always, my parents were there for me. So were my siblings. Even my grandparents. Ryan and some of my other friends ran along the side of the street, sometimes up on the sidewalk, bobbing and weaving through the roadside spectators to keep pace, to share the moment with me.

Almost before I knew it I reached Haywood and passed the flame to the next runner, Lydia Gould, who had been a friend of mine since third grade. She had been selected for her achievements as an outstanding student and a great high school athlete. Lydia gave me a hug, and then I stood watching as she took off with the lighted torch; and the accompanying acclamation moved on. Just that quickly it was over. My moment of Olympic glory—gone forever. Except as I relived it all for the crowd of friends who quickly surrounded and congratulated me and, of course, for the reporters, who wanted a sound bite to describe the experience.

"The whole thing was unbelievable," I told the *Asheville Citizen-Times*. "The idea that this flame's going to Atlanta and it came from Greece and so many people have passed it on, one to the other—it's just indescribable. Nothing can replace these memories—nothing. You can't compare it to anything else, and you can't describe it in any words."

I spent quite a bit of time that summer after I graduated from high school reliving past memories and dreaming about my future. For much of my life I'd felt as though the world viewed me as some kind of monster. Then recently, not just at the Olympic torch relay but with all the other honors and accolades as well, I'd been treated more like a hero.

It was enough to give a guy a schizophrenic self-image. *Which was it? Who am I? Am I the monster people shy away from? Or the hero they line the streets to cheer?*

I was about to leave home and take those questions with me. Wherever I went I knew there would be new people, situations, and circumstances that would take me before crowds I'd never been in before. I knew people were going to stare. And I knew that would hurt.

But in some ways, knowing how people were going to react made it easier for me to face a new challenge. I just had to accept it and walk in. When you can't hide, there's no reason to try. It allows me to be myself, and in that way I realized I was freer than a lot of people I knew.

I walk into any room knowing that everyone will look at me. Some will turn away; to them I'm a monster. Others will look up to me as a hero; to them I'm someone who has gone through a tremendous amount of pain and hardship— and overcome it. Neither reaction is easy to live with.

But when I was tempted to feel sorry for myself, to sink into self-pity, that's when I knew I had to fall back on my faith.

Sure, it's hard to live in the spotlight. Rejection and judgment can be painful. But it isn't easy being a role model either, because you have to live up to the expectations.

Monster or hero? I wasn't sure which was tougher. But I didn't want to change my life because I knew God had allowed me to live for a purpose. And I really believed what I told the Asheville newspaper: "God gave me a blessing instead of shortcoming."

I realized God was still constant— I was still made in his image, and that was what mattered. He would not change.

As I replayed the memories and tried to imagine what lay ahead in the future, I realized God was still constant—I was still made in his image, and that was what mattered. He would not change. He knew what I was capable of and what I wasn't capable of. I didn't have to *do* for him. I didn't have to concern myself with anyone else's view of me but the view that God had of me. I could just *be*. And that whatever I might be, God would be there with me. Always.

My years in high school had been successful and rewarding beyond what I ever imagined. And I had confidence—the best was yet to come!

Chapter 19

On a warm August evening in northcentral Indiana, I sat with my parents in an auditorium crowded with anxious-looking new college students and their parents, waiting to listen to the president of Taylor University, Dr. Jay Kesler, give the freshman orientation address. No doubt some of my future classmates were feeling a little apprehensive. Maybe even sad. But I was excited. This was the night before college! Tomorrow morning, all the parents now present with us would be heading home, and we would be left with each other. I would meet lots of new people and have fun doing it. Studies would come later.

I was waiting for the program to start, anticipating the new experiences lying ahead, when one of the college administrators worked his way down the aisle to the row where I was sitting. He introduced himself and shook my hand. "We'd like you to come up on the platform and say a few words to your fellow classmates."

I was so surprised that I don't remember any of the parameters he gave me in terms of time or topic. My mind was suddenly racing. I didn't feel I could decline the honor. But the program was scheduled to start in two minutes, and I had no idea what I was going to say.

Moments later I found myself sitting up on the platform alongside a college president, staring out at all the strangers seated in front of me. My thoughts still raced. What could I say to my new classmates, many of whom I hoped would become lifelong friends? I'd never been a college freshman before either! What wisdom did I have to share that might help them through the transition that lay ahead for all of us?

Only seconds before I was introduced, I decided what I would say. So when I stepped to the podium, I gave a report on my summer vacation. Sort of . . .

One of my high school graduation gifts was a two-week trip to Alaska with my dad and my grandpa—a real "male bonding" experience. The first week we spent traveling and sightseeing. Week two we fished.

We started out deep-sea fishing for halibut in the Gulf of Alaska. Dad landed several, including a thirty-five-pounder that seemed like a monster. My grandpa caught one that weighed more than twenty pounds. The only halibut I hooked resembled a guppy more than it did the fish my father had caught. So we decided to throw mine back.

I hoped my luck would change when we moved inland to fish for king salmon on the Kenai River. We paid for three spots on a charter fishing boat that motored up that scenic wilderness river, with rich green forests and rugged mountains running alongside the river and bald eagles soaring through the sky overhead.

Relying on the experience of our captain and guide, we trolled upstream and then drifted down, searching for the schools of king salmon that were running that time of year, watching and waiting for the tips of the rods to suddenly bend down and signal a strike.

As the hooks—baited with salmon eggs—dragged along the stony bottom, they often snagged on or between rocks, jerking the rod down before releasing and bobbing free again. Many times I grabbed my fishing rod, anxious to prove my fishing prowess, only to have the hooks pull free from those confounded rocks and leave me to acknowledge yet another false alarm and return to my seat empty-handed.

Before our first day on the river was over, I watched Dad haul in a twenty- to twenty-five-pound king salmon that looked as though it would give him bragging rights to the biggest salmon as well as the prize halibut. Grandpa caught a few small fish, but no kings. Still, he was doing better than I was.

Suddenly my pole bent almost in two. I'd been disappointed so many times that I just knew I'd snagged the bottom again. But when I grabbed the pole, the line bobbed and took off. "Fish on!" I shouted, and everyone else reeled in their lines to give me room. For a while I wondered if I had a fish or a log. Whatever I'd hooked felt heavy enough to drag me overboard.

"I think it's a big one!" the captain assured me. I needed the encouragement because my battle with that salmon soon made my arms feel like lead. When the fish finally surfaced, the captain exclaimed, "Looks like a forty-pounder!" It was huge. Big enough to earn me honors for biggest salmon of the trip, for sure. But every time I got that fish close to the boat, it'd make another run through the deep, glacial-green water. My arms became so tired I was about to hand the rod to my dad when the mate grabbed a net and prepared to land it. Suddenly the line went slack, and my heart sank. It had thrown the hook. I'd lost my trophy. I'd blown my big chance to beat my dad's catch.

I was still trying to shake my disappointment on the second day. If only I hadn't lost that whopper! I had asked the captain what I'd done wrong. He'd told me the problem was getting the big ones hooked solidly. "When you grab the rod and go to set the hook," he said, "try to yank the jaws right out of the fish."

I determined that's what I'd do today—if I got another chance.

Dad caught another one in the thirty- to thirty-five-pound range. Grandpa and I each landed twenty-pounders. Nobody hooked anything as big as the one I'd lost.

The captain was about to call it a day. But I wasn't ready to give up. I was still holding my fishing rod, ready to throw my entire weight into it at the first sign of a bite. My rod tip suddenly bent down. "Fish on," I yelled as I yanked upward for all I was worth. The line seemed to go slack.

"Just a teaser!" the captain said.

"I don't think so," I told him. Again my rod tip bent over like a candy cane, and the fish practically yanked the pole out of my hand. "I guess not!" the captain grinned as he grabbed a long landing net and stood it straight up amidship to signal nearby boats that we had a fish on and that they needed to give us the right-of-way as we tried to land him.

I began reeling this fish in as fast as I could go. Lifting the rod tip high to pull the fish closer, then reeling like crazy till my rod tip was almost touching the water. Heave and reel. Heave and reel. I was not going to waste any time on this one.

Less than five minutes had passed when someone shouted, "There it is!" The fish had surfaced right next to the boat, and it looked like a monster. "That's fifty pounds easy!" the captain judged.

I felt sure I was gonna lose this one too. But this time the mate quickly slipped a net underneath the fish on his first try. It was so heavy he had to lay his whole weight on the long handle of the net just to leverage the fish out of the water. Dad and Grandpa had to help him hoist my fish aboard. Wow! Forty-nine inches long and sixty-three pounds. When we laid it in the icebox, it was two or three times as big as any other salmon caught.

We'd drifted a ways downriver while I was fighting my trophy catch, so the captain started the engines and headed us slowly back upstream. As we worked our way through the small fleet of other charter boats fishing the same waters, our captain called out to his competitors, "This kid just caught a sixty-three-pound king, and he doesn't even have any hands!"

Every time he made that announcement, the fishermen and crews on those other boats turned and looked our way. But I didn't mind those stares at all. In fact, I stood on deck, smiling proudly, even waving occasionally at envious well-wishers who yelled out, "Attaboy!" "All right!" "Way to go, kid!"

It wasn't until later that reality began to sink in. When we docked, Dad had to search for a branch small enough to run through my fish's gills, yet strong enough to bear the weight when we held up the fish between us for the required photos. With our makeshift pole balanced on our shoulders, my fish's tail nearly reached the ground. It was almost as big as I was!

Another fisherman told me about landing a forty-pounder; he said he'd had to fight for over two hours before he could boat it. I knew there was no way I could have held on for two hours. Fortunately, I hadn't had to. Somehow I managed to land my sixty-three-pound salmon in only five minutes. I've got him mounted on the wall at home now. And every time I look at him, I still can't believe it happened. It just seems impossible.

I tell you this Alaska adventure story tonight because we're all about to begin a new four-year adventure. I'm sure that at some point every one of us is going to face a challenge that seems impossible, a situation that requires more than we're capable of giving. When that happens, we're going to need each other. And we will need to remember that God can find a way to provide us the strength we will need to achieve a success even greater than we can dream of.

That was my first introduction to most of my college classmates, and their introduction to me. And even as I walked back to my seat to the applause of the entire audience, I felt I belonged at Taylor University.

I had chosen the school for a number of reasons. I knew I didn't want to be at a big state school. I knew if I were to go there, I would run into the same things every day when new people would see me. With only 2,200 students at Taylor, I figured I could know, and be known by, most of the student body. While it may seem like a serious disadvantage to go to a college surrounded by flat fields of corn as far as you could see, I saw Taylor's rural, somewhat sheltered setting as one of its strengths. I had also decided that Taylor embodied what I wanted most—a school that promised a creative community of young people committed to academic excellence. Along with the school's dedication to faith and learning, there were the family ties. Not only had my parents met there, but my sister Jami would be a senior there during my freshman year.

Speaking to the freshmen during orientation hadn't been my first introduction to the Taylor University campus. Once I had made my choice during my senior year of high school, my parents found a unique way to acquaint me with the campus and vice versa. Mom and Dad didn't send a social worker to show videos the first day, like they had when I started grade school. They didn't go and try to educate the faculty and the dean ahead of time, the way they did before I started junior high. They did something much more effective. They sent me.

I was given the opportunity to introduce myself to the entire college community. It came during the spring semester of my senior year of high school when I spoke at a regular chapel service at Taylor. Chapel took place three times a week and was almost always packed out, despite students and faculty having the option not to attend.

The president, Dr. Jay Kesler, interviewed me on stage in front of a good-sized crowd of my future schoolmates. I remember his first question.

"Joel, why did you choose Taylor University?"

Without hesitation I replied, "Because of the chicks!" As thunderous laughter followed, I remember thinking to myself, *This isn't going to be so bad!*

I received a great response at the time, but the real payoff came that following fall. Because I'd shared my story in that spring chapel, when I showed up with the rest of the freshman class, most of the upperclassmen on campus knew who I was and understood what had happened to me, and they already had a positive attitude toward me. Then I'd had that unexpected opportunity to introduce myself to all my freshman classmates during the orientation meeting. Those two experiences combined gave me a chance to answer most of the questions before they were asked. Plus, they gave me a sense of control over the way I was introduced (and ultimately accepted) on the Taylor University campus.

The other wise thing my parents and I agreed on ahead of time was my roommate situation. Instead of going potluck and just accepting whomever the school paired up with me, we requested a roommate I already knew. Jason Martinson and I had known each other for years at CAMP-of-the-WOODS in New York. Our families had been friends since his dad played football with my dad at Taylor back in the 1960s.

Of course, the fact that we'd been at camp together didn't guarantee we'd be compatible college roommates. I expected there would have to be compromises and adjustments. That's always the case. But at least Jason and I didn't have to deal with the shock or awkwardness of him arriving on campus and being surprised by me. I didn't have to wonder and worry about how long it might take my roommate to look past the scars and see the real me. And I knew I'd have a roommate who wouldn't think it was a big deal when I asked him to knot my necktie or to lace up my tennis shoes.

I'd been so concerned about how well my roommate would adjust to me that I didn't give enough thought ahead of time to the fact that I might need to do some major adjusting of my own.

For example, it took a little time to get used to the fact that Jason was a two-alarm roommate. He was such a sound sleeper that he had to set two different alarms to wake him up so he could get to class on time each morning. If that wasn't annoying enough, he made use of the snooze button on both alarms—every morning, multiple times.

I didn't even know how a snooze button worked before I roomed with Jason. But I soon found out.

One time Jason decided he was going to get up at one in the morning and study the rest of the night for a test he had to take at 8:00 a.m. He set both alarms for 1:00 a.m. I know he did because I heard them go off and promptly woke up in time to hear my roommate hit both snooze buttons. Again. And again. And again.

I didn't say anything to Jason because I was curious to see how long it would take for his two-alarm system to actually get him out of bed. I eventually got tired enough that I pulled the covers over my head and slept through some of the alarms myself. Finally at nine o'clock in the morning I heard an alarm go off, followed by the sound of my roommate's feet hitting the floor and a loud exclamation as he realized what had happened: "Shoot! I missed my eight o'clock class!"

I kept my head covered and tried not to laugh. I couldn't believe it either! Maybe I should have contacted Guinness. My roommate must have set some kind of world record, sleeping through two alarms that went off every nine minutes for eight solid hours. On top of that, he'd missed the class and the test he'd intended to study for all night.

Apart from a few minor adjustments we both had to make, the roommate decision proved a good one. Most, if not all, of the anticipated benefits paid off. Despite our differences, Jason and I did indeed get along well enough that we would room together for two years.

Unfortunately, though, no roommate could have helped me with the biggest problem I confronted that fall. The adjustment to college life is a challenge for most freshmen. Mine was made tougher by what I now realize were the unrealistically high expectations I held—for myself and for Taylor. And for that, I thought my family was at least partially to blame.

My parents had a wonderful college experience on the Taylor campus years before. Not only had they found each other there, but they'd also developed lifelong friendships with students and faculty that had grown deeper and richer over the years. They'd set their life course, vocationally and spiritually, during their college days at Taylor.

Much the same thing had happened with my sister Jami. I'd watched her spend most of her high school years doing what many adolescents do—struggling to find herself. Looking for meaningful relationships and a place to fit in.

No sooner had she started college than it seemed to me that my sister blossomed—spiritually, emotionally, intellectually—into a very impressive young woman. I envied the number of rich relationships she developed with roommates and friends in the dorm.

I had similar goals for my college experience. And since it had all seemed to happen so fast, so effortlessly, for Jami, I expected everything to click the same way for me. When it didn't, I couldn't help wondering what my problem was.

Thoughts and questions like that made me feel uncertain and insecure. And those sorts of feelings helped lead to an experience that, as I remember it, now sounds kind of laughable. But at the time, it seemed to epitomize the struggles I was going through.

One afternoon early that fall of my freshman year some guys I knew asked me if I'd like to join them and a bunch of girls they'd invited to go Rollerblading around campus. At home, if a friend had asked me that, I would have told him I appreciated the invitation. Then I would have explained that in-line skates were even more painful for me than regular roller skates—that despite the operations I'd gone through to give me more flexibility, I simply could not flex my ankles so as to tilt either foot forward enough to stop the way you have to do on Rollerblades. So thanks for asking, but I'll have to pass, and maybe I can do something else with you another time.

However, since I just wanted to fit in and hang out with potential college friends, I didn't want to take the risk of admitting the truth—that it had been a while since I'd skated. *You never know; it might be different this time*, I told myself. So I said, "Sounds great!" and agreed to go.

I borrowed some skates, and six of us guys hiked over to the girls' dorm on the other side of campus. When six freshman girls came out to meet us, I decided I liked the odds.

We all buckled on our skates. But when I stood up, my Rollerblades wheeled right out from under me, and I went down hard. If I hadn't managed to get my arms out and catch myself at the last second, I would have planted my face right in the ground. Only quick reflexes prevented injury to anything but my pride.

"You okay, Joel?"

"Oh, sure." I laughed off any concern. *Well, that's one way to break the ice!* I thought, as I carefully eased myself back to my feet.

"Everybody ready?" someone asked.

A chorus of "yeahs." And we were off.

Just like the roller rink in Black Mountain back in elementary school, there were two basic kinds of skaters. The graceful, smooth, fluid folks who glide at incredible speeds with seemingly little effort and a minimum of moving body parts. And then people like me, skaters who don't so much glide as we stagger on our skates, using every muscle in our bodies to run, oh so awkwardly, and then coast. Of course, everyone else seemed to be gliding as I plodded along at the end of the line—in my distinctly herky-jerky style.

We streamed up and down sidewalks almost continuously from one end of campus to the other. The few times we had to stop, I either coasted to a gradual halt or managed to brake more quickly by stepping off the sidewalk and into the grass.

After twenty or thirty minutes without falling, I began to relax. I don't think I ever got to the gliding stage, but at least I managed to impose something of a rhythm to my movements that made my herky a little less jerky.

Back and forth we zoomed, snaking around buildings, zipping in and out of shadows, at what seemed like faster and faster speeds. Occasionally we bunched up. Other times I felt as though I was racing all-out, trying not to lose sight of the next-to-last person in line.

Looking ahead at one point, I saw our line split. One person zigged left onto a sidewalk, and the next zagged right onto a parallel street. Another left. One more right. Left. Right. Left. Right. Left. I went right.

Barreling down the street now to catch up with my new friends, I suddenly noticed that my entire line was braking to an abrupt stop in the middle of the road just ahead. There was no grass to step off into, but I did manage to swerve and avoid plowing into another skater. I tried my best to come to a complete stop.

My skates did stop momentarily. Then they followed the rest of me as I sailed through the air and gained the instant airborne revelation that I was about to be splattered all over the cement.

No sooner had I given new meaning to the expression "ground to a halt" than I was surrounded by concerned skaters. I gingerly rolled over and slowly sat up to assess the damage. Nothing felt broken. But I'd sustained nasty abrasions the entire length of my body. The worst was a five-inch scrape on my leg that oozed blood.

Within seconds everyone hovered over me in sympathy and concern. Even as I insisted I was going to be fine, I was reminded again of a harsh truth: girls are seldom attracted to blood. Bleeding all over yourself may get you attention—but it's not usually the kind of attention you want.

It was definitely not the kind of impression I'd hoped to make. When I finally limped back to my dorm alone that night, I had no pride left.

Unfortunately, that crash-and-bleed scenario was symbolic of other relationships that freshman year. It seemed the more I wanted close friends who would challenge me spiritually and intellectually, the harder I tried to find them. And the harder I tried, the harder I failed. I began to struggle with doubts.

My sister Jami was a beautiful young woman, and relationships in college came easier for her. Everybody in our culture, even among Christians, knows that appearance matters. Maybe that was the problem.

Part of me wondered if the reason I struggled in the relationship arena at college was the residence I lived in. Bergwall Hall did have a reputation as something of a "nerd dorm." Maybe if I had been in one of the "cooler" residences, where most of the jocks or popular crowd hung out, it would have been easier to find quality relationships.

Still, I put on a happy, friendly face, made a point of cheerfully greeting people everywhere I went on campus, and got involved in things—on and off campus—that exercised my leadership abilities. I joined the Inter-class Council (ICC) at Taylor and was elected president of my sophomore class. I accepted an invitation to be a keynote speaker at the World Burn Congress VII held in Philadelphia during my sophomore year. I also delivered a keynote address for several hundred students at a missions conference held in Gatlinburg, Tennessee, in the spring that year.

But perhaps the single most significant development in my life during those first couple years of college had nothing to do with school. It began with a shocking phone call just a few days after I got home for the summer after my first year at Taylor.

When Mom walked in the door after work on June 5, 1997, she hit the replay button on the telephone answering machine. A man's voice said, "Mrs. Sonnenberg, this is Roger Talbot from the Manchester *Union Leader* [newspaper]. They picked up the truck driver responsible for your son's injuries . . ."

Mom froze and exclaimed, "Oh, my goodness!" Then she began to cry.

She rushed up to my room a few minutes later and interrupted a phone conversation I was having with a friend to announce, "Joel! You'll never guess what happened!"

There was a somberness to her tone that got my immediate attention. The look on her face and her agitated manner underscored the seriousness of her words.

"What?" I responded.

"They arrested Reginald Dort!" Seeing the blank look on my face, she added, "The truck driver who caused our accident!"

"Really?"

The implications didn't hit me as hard or as quickly as they had my mother. The idea took a few minutes to sink in. And then I still didn't know what it all meant.

For a long while, none of us did. But we began to get hints the very next day.

Chapter 20

The front-page headline in the June 6 edition of Manchester, New Hampshire's, *Union Leader* proclaimed, "Runaway Trucker Arrested After 18 Years."* The article, written by the reporter who'd left his name on our answering machine the day before, began this way:

A Canadian trucker who ran away almost 18 years ago will return to New Hampshire to face charges stemming from a fiery tollbooth crash that took Joel Sonnenberg's fingers, toes and left hand, his eyelids, nose, lips and ears, and burned deep into his skull.

Reginald Henry Dort, 49, was jailed in Illinois yesterday, awaiting a police escort to New Hampshire.

"We are in the process of trying to extradite Mr. Dort from Illinois to New Hampshire," said assistant Rockingham County attorney Tracey Connelly.

At a hearing in Rock Island County Circuit Court on Wednesday, Dort "decided to waive extradition and return to New Hampshire," said his lawyer, Frank Fuhr, of Rock Island, Illinois.

Dort, who was driving for an Ontario-based company, was arrested when officers at a truck scale in Illinois ran his name through their computer, Fuhr said.

Up popped his arrest warrant New Hampshire authorities had entered into the National Crime Information Center's files after Dort forfeited $1,000 bail and fled to Canada in 1979. That year a Rockingham

*"Runaway Trucker Arrested After 18 Years," *The Union Leader*, June 6, 1997. Copyright © 1997, *The Union Leader*, Manchester, N.H. Reprinted with permission.

County grand jury had indicted Dort for second-degree assault, a felony punishable on conviction by up to seven years in prison. He was charged with operating an 18-wheel tractor trailer "in heavy traffic conditions at an excessive rate of speed" as he approached the Interstate 95 northbound toll plaza at Hampton on September 15, 1979.

The 81,000-pound onion-laden truck Dort was driving collided with six cars, including a 1973 Chevrolet in which 22-month-old Joel Sonnenberg sat strapped in a car seat. . . .

The article went on to summarize what had happened to me and included a couple of quotes from our old friend Nancy McKenzie, telling about where my family and I were and recounting some of my high school and college achievements. But there was no more information on Dort or his arrest. Those details would trickle in over the days and weeks and months that followed.

Eventually, Dort was transported from Illinois back to New Hampshire, where later that summer he was charged with at least nine counts of second-degree assault and faced additional charges for jumping bail and fleeing prosecution eighteen years earlier. He was going nowhere this time. The judge found him a flight risk and ordered him held in custody until trial on a $500,000 cash bail.

As a family we talked about the implications. One day I told my mother, "If it was up to me, Mom, I wouldn't want to string this guy up."

Mom told me, "Think about what your life would have been like, Joel, if you wouldn't have been burned. I really want you to think about that!"

"Stop it, Mom!" I told her. "I can't even think that way! I have no idea what it would be like not to have been burned. . . . I want you to think—think about all the things I wouldn't have done if I hadn't been burned. I have done so much more—I'm doing so much more—than I'd be doing if I was just like everyone else."

I had to think like that. I didn't know another way.

If I ever felt any anger toward Reginald Dort, I think it was more over the pain and grief he'd caused my family through the years than over what he'd done to me. I'd never known any other existence.

My parents had every reason to be bitter and vengeful. But they weren't. I think God had enabled them to let those feelings go years before. I don't remember a single mention of Reginald Dort's name in our home while I was growing up. I know from time to time they wondered, as I did, what ever had happened to him. But they never obsessed about it. And now that he'd been caught, he still wasn't a frequent subject of conversation.

When I expressed my own reservations about seeing him punished, my folks did remind me that "it's not going to be us trying him. It's the state of New Hampshire."

"All people who do things wrong need forgiveness," Dad would tell me— and he would say the same thing to any reporter who asked. "That's what we believe as Christians. And we need to forgive him as well. But there needs to be some justice. Even though there could never be enough justice for what Joel has gone through."

When reporters asked if we'd be attending the trial, we told them we had no such plans. But I did tell the *Asheville Citizen-Times*, "I think I'd like to talk to him. Man-to-man. I'd like that closure because he's played a big part in my life, whether I like it or not. He's put me through a lot of pain, but what he did has also made me the person I am."

The wheels of justice do grind slowly. A trial date was set for some months off. Before it arrived, we got word that Dort had pleaded guilty to one count of second-degree assault. The prosecutors had accepted the plea bargain because they were finding it difficult to put together a solid case when so many of the principles, including witnesses and victims, had moved or disappeared in the twenty years since the accident. They chose to avoid the expense and the uncertainty of a trial—knowing the plea bargain would at least result in some jail time for the accused.

No one knew how long a sentence Reginald Dort would receive. That would be up to the judge, who set a sentencing hearing for the July after my sophomore year at Taylor.

Once that news was released, and especially after my family and I were subpoenaed to appear at the sentencing hearing, the media swarm began. Not only did we receive phone calls from reporters at papers around the country, but our old friend Carol Marin and her producer Don Mosely called and asked permission to go with us to New Hampshire to film the conclusion of the story they'd been following for almost fourteen years. (Carol had made headlines of her own a few months before. She'd taken a stand for journalistic integrity and resigned her lucrative anchor position at NBC's Chicago affiliate and found work as a reporter for CBS rather than share her evening news set with tabloid talk-show host Jerry Springer, who'd been hired by station management in a controversial ploy to boost ratings.)

Once she'd learned what was happening in my life, Carol had pitched the story idea to another former NBC star who'd also jumped to CBS. When she asked Bryant Gumbel if he'd like a piece for his newsmagazine show, *Public Eye*, he immediately recalled the previous stories Carol had done for the *Today* show. "Are you kidding?" he responded. "Of course I'm interested!"

On a beautiful summer day in mid-July, Mom, Dad, my little brother Kyle, and I climbed into our SUV and headed north toward New Hampshire. Sommer and Jami would join us there a couple days later. And together our family would face for the first time the man who had so greatly impacted all of our lives.

The CBS cameras traveled with us—sometimes following behind, other times riding in the vehicle with us.

Mom and Dad reminisced as we sped along I-95 north toward the Hampton toll plaza where the accident had taken place. Kyle informed us that there was an 18-wheeler behind us as we slowed to pay our toll. "We were in the far right-hand lane weren't we, Mike?" Mom asked. Dad agreed with her memory, and we all fell silent as we rolled to a stop and Dad handed his money to the attendant.

A short while later we pulled up in front of the courthouse in Brentwood, New Hampshire. We were welcomed warmly by a court-appointed victim advocate, who took us inside. When we sat down and talked with the prosecutors before the hearing, they explained again the challenges they had faced in gathering the necessary evidence and testimony to reconstruct the nearly twenty-year-old case.

But they made sure we understood what they had pieced together. Dort had claimed his brakes had failed, but the accident investigators determined there was nothing wrong with his brakes. They also confirmed what we'd heard about Dort knowing the woman in the first car he hit. So the investigators and prosecutors speculated that the entire accident happened because he was trying to forcibly stop this woman—someone with whom he'd had some kind of relationship. Very possibly he was trying to keep her from going to Canada and confronting his wife and family.

The woman insisted to investigators that she had never had any kind of romantic relationship with Dort. And she was unable to testify as to what happened that day at the toll plaza because, she claimed, ever since the accident she had suffered from amnesia that had wiped out her memory of the crash and the entire day preceding it.

This part of the mystery remains. So we may never know the answer to "Why?" But that was only a small disappointment in what was otherwise a rather memorable and meaningful day for the Sonnenberg family.

A few minutes prior to the scheduled hearing our family was escorted into the courtroom of Superior Court Judge Douglas R. Gray. Moments later we got our first glimpse of Reginald Dort, a tall, thin, graying man wearing an orange prison jumpsuit and led by deputies to the defense table, where he took his seat between a pair of court-appointed public defenders.

We all stood when the bailiff announced the judge's entrance. And when we'd sat back down, the judge gaveled the hearing to order. The facts of the case, the official charges, and the details of the pleading were all briefly reviewed. But before the judge pronounced his sentence, every member of our family (other than Kyle) was given a few minutes to say whatever we wanted with regard to the case or the punishment we thought Reginald Dort deserved.

My sister Sommer went to the podium first, facing the judge and the defense table. This is what she told the court:

I come as a member of a family that has suffered and endured greatly over the past eighteen years. I come into court this morning with a perspective unlike any other. I know no "before" the accident; I only know "after" the accident. So I didn't know Joel with hair, smooth skin, fingers, or toes. I've only known Joel as he comes before you this morning.

. . . watching Joel spend countless hours in the hospital . . . seeing the physical pain during and after the hospital visits . . . and the emotional pain—the stares . . . the constant explanations . . . the frequent absence of my parents and the attention regularly directed to the needs of Joel. . . .

Justice cannot be served this morning. No jail sentence can take back all that Joel or that my family has been through.

My parents have witnessed to me the power of the cross. And with Christ as the center of my life, and through his love and his forgiveness,

I can love and forgive him who has done this wrong to my family. Yet this does not justify his actions.

Thanks, Mom and Dad, for your love and support. And thank you, Joel, for showing me true beauty.

I think the whole family was sniffling and wiping our eyes by the time Sommer finished and Jami took her place:

At twenty years of age I have already had a unique life. On that September day back in 1979, my family changed forever. Instantaneously. We had no choice. It was then, at three years of age, I began my atypical childhood with numerous trips to the hospital ... witnessing my brother screaming during dressing changes ... the absence of my parents....

Although I never stopped being a daddy's girl, Joel's needs were always more pressing, more urgent.

Explaining my brother's disfigurements to my friends became tedious. I always became frustrated, because their acceptance of Joel took longer than I wanted it to. It was hard to comprehend why others had such a problem with my little brother just because he looked different.

I grew up quickly because of the accident. I learned to be strong and stand tall when others laughed and stared at my brother. I also found that my place in the family was not to be in the limelight; I was to be backstage support.

While I was experiencing all of this, my parents were going through their own hardships and struggles. I have seen firsthand that, when something traumatic happens to family, it turns the family unit inside out. Every little feeling seems to be exposed.

I am so grateful for my parents and their leadership of our family. They were always giving of themselves. Mom and Dad showed us what forgiveness is all about, and they showed us that a positive, never-give-up attitude goes an awfully long way.

Joel's life is different in almost every way imaginable. What he has gone through since that day here in New Hampshire is incomprehensible to me.... There isn't an amount of jail time that can make up for what he has lost and gone through....

Joel, I admire your perseverance, your go-get-'em attitude, your love of life, and, most important, your reliance on Jesus Christ. Thank you for teaching me what's really important in life.

Thank you, Mom and Dad, for teaching us that no matter what terrible thing is thrown our way—if we choose to abide in the Lord and have a smile on our face and joy in our heart—everything can be conquered eventually.

My mom followed Jami. And she began by addressing the court:

Your Honor, I would like to express to the court that my family and I are thrilled with the plea bargain agreement the court and Mr. Dort have made. We are relieved that the minute details of the horrendous accident at the Hampton tollbooths almost nineteen years ago do not have to be relived [here] in an extended trial. We are relieved that Mr. Dort has pled guilty to the charges.

However, the details have been relived by this mother over and over and over again throughout these years. . . .

You have heard about, in very general terms, a very small fraction of [Joel's] pain. As a mother, I have lived his pain, caused some of his pain, and have attempted to relieve his pain in any way I possibly can.

I could describe for you today all the physical care for my son over the last nineteen years—dressing changes of muscle layers covered with grafted skin, an exposed skull the size of a baseball hat on his head, creams, lotions, medicine, hospitalizations, and tremendous managerial tasks for parents having to coordinate the care of our son and our family.

Of all the anguishing moments, perhaps the most difficult were the searching questions of a growing boy to his mother: At the age of four—"Mama, will my skin ever be smooth and soft like yours?" Joel at age five—"Mama, when will I have fingers?" (Like they were teeth that would grow in.) At age eight—"Why did that truck hit us, Mom? Why didn't he stop?" Joel at fifteen—"Mom, I think I've suffered more than Jesus did on the cross."

Your Honor, nothing can replace what my son has lost physically. We have lived from the first moment for heaven, and what it will mean for

Joel—the complete elimination of pain and suffering, and a glorious new body which cannot be destroyed. The beauty of what we've experienced is that evil has turned into good—God has turned the worst devastation into beauty, into a powerful story that he is using for his own purposes. Today I give him all the praise for accomplishing so very much in Joel's life, and in ours.

I forgive Mr. Dort of his negligence and his destructive act. I plead with him to listen to the voice of his Maker . . . to see himself as God sees him, scarred just like Joel, only on the inside. But the Lord can make him whole with a new and purposeful life.

"The beauty of what we've experienced is that evil has turned into good—God has turned the worst devastation into beauty, into a powerful story that he is using for his own purposes."

After Mom returned to her seat, they called Dad to the podium. He too thanked the court and expressed his belief that justice was being served—even if true justice could not yet be accomplished.

He then described two representative days to remind the court and Mr. Dort what our family had been through. He first recounted the physical ordeal he'd endured in the hospital after the accident. How he'd been confined to bed by his own burns as each day people would report the number of fingers and toes that I had lost. How what little life I had left was being lost finger by finger. "I couldn't see my son," Dad said. "I didn't know whether to pray that he would live or die. I was crushed to the depth of my soul. But my pain would pale compared to Joel's pain."

At that point Dad switched gears and described in detail one of my horribly painful dressing changes from the age of four or five. Then he drew this conclusion:

We have lost a lot as a family. We have suffered as a family, but Joel has suffered the most. I have come here not so much for punishment for Mr. Dort—because we all make mistakes and have to pay the consequences. But, Mr. Dort, I have come here to hear you say you are sorry. When you ask for my forgiveness, I will forgive, but I cannot forget. When you ask Jesus for forgiveness, he will forgive and forget.

Eighteen years ago you walked to freedom; we were restricted to the confines of the hospital and rehab clinics.

In the past eighteen years you combed your hair, while we changed bandages on my son's hairless head.

In the past eighteen years you laughed, while we cried buckets of tears.

In the past eighteen years you have tied your shoes, while we had to tie Joel's shoes.

In the past eighteen years you had time for friends, while we had barely enough time for each other.

In the past eighteen years you planned your future, while we barely planned a day.

Eighteen years ago you lived, while Joel struggled to live and almost died.

Mr. Dort, eighteen years ago you took a bouncing, vibrant baby and gave me back a smoldering, screaming lump of coal. Through the years the pressure, the cutting, and the polishing of the doctors, friends, family, and God has transformed this lump of coal of no apparent value into a sparkling diamond of rarest beauty and untold worth.

I give to you my son, Joel.

As Dad returned to his seat, I stood and bear-hugged him for what seemed an eternity. Then, as we both wiped the tears from our eyes, he sat down and I walked to the front of that courtroom and finally faced the man whose crime had so impacted my life. I opened my notebook and began to read from my notes. My voice cracked on the first few words, and I wondered if I was going to be able to get through this. But I could almost feel God giving me strength as I continued:

It is my understanding that you, Mr. Reginald Dort, have conveniently forgotten about me for the past nineteen years. As you have heard, during [that time] my family and I have suffered immensely, while you, Mr. Dort, continued to drive a truck in Canada.

I have no recollection of September 15, 1979. The earliest memories I have are of growing up in a hospital where I experienced every child's nightmare of being alone and helpless. Those memories continue to haunt me to this day. . . .

The only form of power I had was in my voice, screaming, crying, and many times pleading, "Please be gentle! Be gentle! Be gentle!" Also I remember times at night, when my parents had to leave, being left alone in a dark hospital ward with no one to talk to, surrounded by crying children.

At the very least, you, Mr. Dort, robbed me of my childhood. But what you could not steal were the thousands of prayers people prayed for our family. . . . The ceiling above my hospital bed was blanketed with colorful cards that poured in from around the world—each signifying people who were praying for me. This love, shown to me in countless ways, would follow me for the years to come. . . .

Ever since the accident, I have grown up into a world that does not welcome me. At first glance, I seem anything but human. Anywhere outside the confines of my home I am vulnerable for attack. Suffocating stares and countless comments like, "Look at that!" "Take off your mask!" "Yuck!"

Imagine for a moment the most embarrassing characteristic about yourself—something you know is not normal. Now I want you to take whatever you thought of and write it in BIG BOLD letters on a poster board and wear it for the rest of your life. Imagine going to the mall, where everyone would see your poster board. This is not a dream; this is my reality.

For me, Disney World seems more like hell than a wonderland. Going for a relaxing time at the movies is far from relaxing. Every comment and reaction imaginable has taken place in the first twenty years of my life. . . .

I am still learning to smile at people's curiosity and intrigue. I have to deal with tough questions like, *Who am I? Will I ever get married? How can I continue to relate to people when they laugh at me? How do I remain positive?*

It's a wonder how I maintain the sanity that I have left.

Many say, "Well, Joel, you have tremendous strength." Yet I would be helpless on my own. "Well, Joel, you have a great family." Yet they would be the first to admit they would be hopeless without the power of prayer. . . .

Second Corinthians 12:9 tells us, "My grace is sufficient for you, for my strength is made perfect in weakness." It is amazing to have this revealed in our own lives. That the Lord can turn such a blatant weakness into a strength is a miracle. It cannot be described any other way.

Today the surgeries have subsided. But I have had nearly fifty surgeries and have spent over two years of my life in the hospital. . . .

Where is there justice for a lifetime of pain and suffering? Where is there justice for all wrongdoings? . . . For my family and me, justice will not exist in this courtroom today. But complete and perfect justice does exist. It will exist when I step outside of this courtroom. It will exist when my family and I will be able to carry on with our lives.

This is my prayer for you, Mr. Reginald Dort, that you may know that our Lord and Savior Jesus Christ's grace has no limits and the world does not make sense without him. Because he first loved us.

We will not consume our lives with hatred, because hatred only brings misery. Yet we will surround ourselves with love—unconditional love in God's grace.

> "We will not consume our lives with hatred, because hatred only brings misery. Yet we will surround ourselves with love—unconditional love in God's grace."

With that I closed my notebook, looked one more time at Reginald Dort, who had his head down, and walked back to my seat.

Moments later Judge Gray asked the defendant to rise. Reginald Dort stood between his lawyers as the judge pronounced a sentence of three years in a New Hampshire state correctional facility. He first asked if the defendant understood the sentence and then inquired if Mr. Dort had anything he wished to say. Dort's lawyer told the court that her client understood and accepted the sentence but that he was an uneducated man who didn't feel his words would be adequate to address the court.

Judge Gray peered down from his bench and said, "It doesn't take much to say you're sorry."

"I'm sorry, Your Honor," Dort replied.

"Don't say it to me!" admonished the judge.

Dort turned and faced us for the first time to repeat the words, "I'm sorry."

Then the judge looked at us and said, "To the Sonnenbergs, you've sure got some guts, I'll say that." And he banged his gavel to end the hearing.

That was it. The close of a chapter that had begun more than eighteen years before. The whole ordeal was finally over.

At least I thought it was over.

Chapter 21

If I had ever thought that what happened in the courtroom could relegate Reginald Dort, the accident, and everything I'd been through to the past—never to be spoken of or thought about again—I learned different the minute I walked out into the courthouse hallway. We'd closed nothing. Indeed, we seemed to have opened a floodgate.

Reporters swarmed around from everywhere. Newspapers and magazines around the country picked up and ran with the story.

No sooner did the first wave of follow-up stories begin to die down than CBS's *Public Eye* devoted almost the entire sixty minutes of its July 29, 1998, broadcast to the story. Carol Marin's finished piece recounted the accident itself, documented my recovery over the years, portrayed my life at home and in college today, then climaxed with our family's on-camera courtroom confrontation with Reginald Dort at the sentencing hearing. The result was such a powerful piece of television journalism that the broadcast won both an Emmy Award and the prestigious Peabody Award.

But long before those honors were announced, my family realized the impact the broadcast had on viewers. Not only was there yet another flood of follow-up media coverage (articles and interviews), but the Sonnenberg home was deluged with mail. We heard from family, friends, and complete strangers, who wrote to tell us what the program had meant to them, how much it had inspired them, and how their lives had been impacted by what they'd seen and heard. One such letter, which came from a very surprising source, began:

Dear Mr. and Mrs. Sonnenberg and Family,

As the judge in any case, I am supposed to sit there rather stoically and do my job with dispassion. So this is probably the first letter I ever have written, or ever will write, to anyone appearing in my court.

I am compelled, however, to write to you as a family and express my personal admiration for all of you. Seldom do victims' statements affect either others or me in a courtroom as yours did.

Every person who entered the courtroom that day, including Mr. Dort, left it as a better person because of the presence of all of you.

The personal courage and ethical values you all expressed have had a profound effect on everyone there. I say without hesitation that you have shown everyone here, as well as those watching CBS last night, what a family is all about.

You are indeed a very remarkable family, and I have been honored that you graced my courtroom one day in July 1998.

I wish you all the best in the years ahead, and I shall not forget that day when you showed us all the best side of human nature and family values.

> *With deep respect,*
> *Douglas R. Gray*

The outpouring of affirmation in so many letters humbled us. But it also heartened us to see how, once again, God had used our terrible experience for his (and others') good.

Everywhere I went for those next few weeks, whether at home in North Carolina, on vacation in New York, or back at school in Indiana, people who had seen the broadcast recognized me—and wanted to ask me about it.

For example, soon after the *Public Eye* piece ran, a family friend from church, a guy named Mark, who was running for local political office, invited Dad and me to Asheville for a political fund-raiser/reception. The event was being held in honor of United States Senator Lauch Faircloth, who was campaigning for reelection in North Carolina that year. Dad had some other commitment, but he suggested that I go and that I take Ryan with me in his place. Frankly, I was none too thrilled at the prospect of attending a big public event, but Dad thought it could be an educational experience for me. I still wasn't convinced. Only after he assured me that there would be plenty of free food, and very good food at that, did I agree to go.

The minute we walked into the reception, a seemingly endless line of strangers started filing up to greet me. "Hi, Joel. You don't know me. But I saw the program on television the other night, and I have to tell you . . ."

"Hey, Joel. Great job on TV the other night."

"Our sister-in-law taught out at Black Mountain when you were in grade school. You weren't in her class, so you may not remember her. But we heard so much about you."

"My name's _____, Joel. I want to tell you what an inspiration you are."

"Joel, I'm so excited to finally meet you. I've followed your story in the Asheville paper for years."

I'd shaken so many hands by the time the candidate showed up that I started thinking, *Maybe I should be running for something!*

Senator Faircloth finally arrived with two special celebrity supporters in tow—onetime Republican presidential nominee Senator Bob Dole and professional wrestling star Rick Flair. All three men were scheduled to speak.

My friend Mark was especially keen on meeting Mr. Dole, who spoke first and had to leave early to get to another engagement. So when the senator concluded his remarks and began working his way through the crowd, we ducked through a rear exit and waited outside, hoping to speak with him on his way to his car.

He made it out a few moments later and headed our way. When he spotted me, he immediately walked over. I could hardly believe it, but Senator Dole warmly greeted me by name and said he'd seen the program on television the other night. As he shook my right hand with his left, I was reminded that his right hand had been partially paralyzed, and I later wondered if his disability was the reason he seemed to feel a connection with me. After we talked for another minute or two, he told me, "If there's ever anything I can do for you, Joel, just let me know." Then he shook hands with Ryan and Mark, bid us good-bye, and took off—leaving me to wonder if there was anyone in the country who had not seen me on *Public Eye*.

So many people had so many wonderful things to say after the program aired that I soon had more "encouragement" than I knew what to do with. The people who made the comments had only the best intentions. Both their responses to the network broadcast and their desire to commend me were certainly understandable under the circumstances.

Of course there were unintentional humorous outcomes as well. I did keep a running tally on how many marriage proposals I received in the mail. The last number I remember was four or five. As I told this to friends at school, I would laugh and quote *Dumb and Dumber*: "So you're telling me there's a chance!"

On one level I enjoyed the positive attention, but on another level it was hard for me to understand. Going from people making fun of me at the malls to receiving marriage proposals in the mail seemed to be on two opposite ends of the spectrum.

Yet I was the same person I'd always been.

Sometimes when the TV show and the subject of what a "great example" I was came up, I wanted to say, *Wait just a minute here. Forgiving Reginald Dort wasn't that hard; it was a test-tube case in a very controlled environment. Applying forgiveness in everyday life is much tougher. Getting ticked off at whoever misplaced the remote control for the television. Yelling at my mom for accidentally throwing my favorite white dress shirt in with a load of red clothes and dyeing it pink. That's when I struggle with the practical application of forgiveness. And if you really knew me, you'd know that.*

In the wake of the *Public Eye* broadcast, as I struggled to know how to deal with all the "encouragement" people were giving me, I sought wisdom, insight, and counsel from someone I thought probably knew a little about what it was like to try to live in the spotlight, to be a "public figure"—whether he wanted to be or not. I made an appointment to talk with Taylor University's president, Dr. Jay Kesler.

I began by telling Jay (that's what he wanted students to call him) how I was struggling to accept so much praise and encouragement from people who had seen the television broadcast. I gave him several examples. I explained my reactions and my feelings about those reactions.

After he'd listened for a while, he said, "Joel, during your years as a student here at Taylor, you've probably impacted more lives than most of our graduates could in an entire lifetime . . ."

"Jay," I interrupted, "you're not helping." We both laughed, but I remember thinking, *Wow! Can that really be true? Does Jay really mean that?*

He went on to talk about the power of the media in our society, about how people are influenced by it and how it bestows image and power on people in ways those individuals have no control over. (I knew how that felt!)

He suggested that I needed to consider such attention and acclaim as undeserved honor. Then he added, "God has definitely given you a unique platform, Joel."

I certainly believed that. And I found both reassurance and challenge in the rest of what Jay told me that day: "I don't know what career path God is laying out for you, but I have no doubt that he does have a plan for you, Joel. He has clearly given you many gifts. So you can be certain that, wherever it is he wants to take you, he will continue to use you in an unusual and special way."

I don't know how much Jay's words helped me cope with the ongoing reactions to the television broadcast, but it certainly did help as I began to think more about the future, career plans, and so on. His confident assurance that God had a special plan for me still gave me a real sense of comfort as I gradually came to discover that God was more interested in a personal relationship with me than a place for me to go.

> *God knew the unedited me. Inside and out. He knew everything about me. Yet he loved me anyway.*

It was during this same emotionally difficult time that God seemed to draw especially close. In the Bible God says, "Do not fear, for I have redeemed you; I have called you by name; you are Mine! When you pass through the waters, I will be with you" (Isaiah 43:1–2 NASB). He wasn't fooled by any picture on a television program. He knew the unedited me. Inside and out. He knew everything about me. Yet he loved me anyway.

There's a difference in thinking that and knowing that. I knew. And it made me incredibly grateful to realize I had a personal relationship with the Creator of the universe—the One who loved me.

So once again I learned that it truly didn't matter what other people thought. They weren't the audience I was supposed to live for. I had only one real audience. And if I had a relationship that pleased *him*, that was what really mattered.

When I better understood what and Who I was living for, I better understood the whys of life. But as those truths began to sink in, I found myself less concerned than ever about my limitations, less worried about other people's reactions to me, more content with who I was, more hopeful about where I was going, and more determined than ever to strengthen all my relationships—not just with God but with the people around me.

Eventually I began to see more connections between my relationship with God and my relationships with others. I'd come to college wanting and expecting to see significant progress in both. Here again I was using my sister's experience as a measuring stick. I, too, wanted to grow as a person—spiritually as well as relationally. I didn't want to be the same person I'd always been. I wanted a more consistent, better quiet time with the Lord. I wanted to be more disciplined. And one reason I longed for deeper relationships was because I wanted a close community of peers to whom I could be accountable. Personally. Spiritually.

I spent a year searching and trying to make it happen. And that was a big part of the problem. I was trying. And the harder I worked, the less fruit I saw.

By now you know I'm a 150 percent kind of guy. Where there's a will, there's a way. By the grace of God, I've accomplished a lot in my life through sheer effort and determination. So it took me a long time to realize I couldn't make myself grow. I simply couldn't do it myself.

It required patience. Patience. I don't even like the sound of that word. Let alone its implications.

I was at an excellent school, and I had done all I could do to find my ideal friends. I decided I would begin my sophomore year with the promise that I didn't want anyone to go through what I had gone through my first year. So I made it my duty to be intentional with every underclassman on my floor. I hung out as much as possible with them. We ate meals together in the cafeteria, played intramurals, went camping, played video games, and hung out on the weekends.

Then sometime during the last half of my sophomore year it hit me. Ever since I'd arrived at Taylor, I had been diligently looking everywhere for lasting meaningful relationships. Now I suddenly noticed (maybe God had been trying to show me all along, and I just wasn't paying attention) the potential relationships were all around me. Starting with the guys on my hall. If I wanted to have real friendships, I needed to be a real friend. Did I want to be a leader? I needed to lead from where I was.

And that's what happened. After being a follower and getting into trouble earlier in my life, and after being such a visible, up-front leader in high school and accumulating a lot of recognition for being so "successful," I was finally learning the importance of leading through serving.

Another leadership position in college came when I accepted the role of discipleship coordinator for thirty-seven guys on my dorm floor. Trying to help them grow spiritually forced me to grow. So we grew together. Closer to God. And closer to each other.

Attendance had slowly fallen off at our weekly floor prayer meeting. So I instituted a weekly event called "Prayers and Spares." First we'd get together to share concerns and pray for each other; then we'd all go out to the local lanes, where you could rent shoes for a dollar and bowl for a buck a game.

We held some retreats and did a few other things to specifically foster spiritual growth. But mostly we sponsored activities that encouraged interaction among all the guys on our floor. For example, I asked for and received a bread machine on my twentieth birthday. After that I regularly baked bread in my room. You'd be amazed at what a crowd you can draw with the smell of hot, fresh, homemade bread wafting down the hall of a boys' dorm late at night. Anyone was welcome in my room when I made bread. My roommates and I had only one rule: if you wanted a piece of bread, you had to be willing to sit down and talk while you ate it. It was amazing how many meaningful conversations there were among the guys I broke bread with in my dorm room. Many of those conversations lasted well into the wee hours of the morning.

Not all of our interactions were particularly deep or spiritual. The guys on my hall engaged in a lot of typical college stunts—staging water balloon fights and stuffing cars full of wadded-up newspapers. And since Bergwall Hall didn't have a lot of dorm traditions, we created a few of our own. For example, those of us who didn't have dates on Friday nights (usually the majority of us) would go out and play tennis together. I'd never been very competitive at tennis because it took both arms for me to hold and swing a tennis racket. But I was always up for some fun and a laugh or two, so I figured out a quick way to improve my game. I borrowed an old tennis racket from one of the other guys, and we duct-taped it to my right arm and hand. I still wasn't ready for Wimbledon, but the very first time I tried out my duct-tape strategy, my tennis game did greatly improve. I also learned it would be a really good idea to pull an old tube sock over my hand and arm the next time I used half a roll of duct tape to attach anything to my arm.

Duct tape played an important role in yet another dorm activity. Intramural sports were big at Taylor University. Every dorm on campus participated in a wide variety of competitions—none bigger than the annual flag football league. I was quick enough to get to almost any opposing runner. But because I was at an admitted disadvantage when it came to grabbing a flag, I could do little more than disrupt and slow down a play until a teammate could catch up and make the tackle. Until someone came up with the brilliant idea of wrapping duct tape—sticky side out—around both my arms. I don't know that I grabbed a lot more flags than I had before, but I sure looked more intimidating.

With or without duct tape, there was one other advantage I could provide my flag football team. Instead of a coin toss at the beginning of a game to determine which team would kick off, the team representatives played a quick round of "rock, scissors, paper." I represented our team because my right hand could always beat whatever my opponent put out. If he held out paper, I'd wiggle my thumb to signify scissors. If he held out rock, I'd place my open "hand" over his fist and say, "Paper." And if he threw out two fingers for scissors, I'd raise my hand (which I could never close in an actual fist) and hammer it down on his scissors, saying, "Rock!"

I never lost a game. Which my teammates and I thought was a hoot, because once our opponents agreed to the challenge, there was no going back.

In addition to all the fun and games, several of us in our hall wanted to build a tradition of service—on campus and in the community. So I codirected a Big Brothers/Big Sisters youth program on campus in which a bunch of the guys from our dorm took part. During the Christmas and Easter seasons a group of guys from the floor would go sing carols and hymns and then just sit and visit with some of the folks at a local nursing home.

Perhaps the most unique community outreach occurred when our dorm adopted Mississinewa High School in nearby Gas City, Indiana, as our away-from-home alma mater. We went en masse to many of the school's ball games. We dressed in crazy costumes, sat in their student section, cheered like fanatics for the Mississinewa River Rats (yes, I did say River Rats), and generally did whatever we could to boost school spirit. We'd tailgate in the school parking lot before football games and create our own cheers for the players (and even the water boy). The other Mississinewa fans, the students, and the school staff didn't know what to think the first time forty strangers dressed in outlandish outfits marched into the school's gym and sat together among the other River Rats boosters and cheered fanatically for their basketball team. But they quickly warmed to us and were soon making requests such as, "My son is number 35. Could you guys do a cheer just for him?" or, "The cheerleader on the right end is my daughter, and today's her birthday. Could you boys sing 'Happy Birthday' to her during the next time-out?"

Before long, the school and the community were so glad to have us that, when their basketball team made the state playoffs during my senior year, the athletic director provided an entire school bus just to make sure our Bergwall gang had transportation to the game. And we had other Taylor students—guys and girls from other dorms—asking if they could go along and be a part of our tradition.

One time when the dorms held an open house, our hall decided we'd decorate with a Mississinewa theme. We set up one part of the hallway to look like the main street in downtown Gas City. We even went to the town's public works department and borrowed genuine (old or unused) street signs to add to the effect. The remainder of the hall represented Mississinewa High School itself. We parked an actual MHS bus in front of our dorm and decorated a number of rooms to represent classrooms, the principal's office, and even the school nurse's station. We turned our study lounge into a high school cafeteria, and one of the other guys' moms played the role of lunchroom lady and served sloppy joes to our guests.

Not only did our open house bring a huge turnout of Taylor students; we had distributed flyers at MHS games, and a number of high schoolers showed up to hang out with us at our open house. Everyone had a blast.

Thirty-five of the thirty-seven guys on my floor came home with me to North Carolina for fall break. We all stayed with my family. Guys slept on the floors all throughout the house. Everyone raved about Mom's home cooking. I introduced them to Ryan. And we all spent as many daylight hours together as possible, exploring the Great Smoky Mountains together—hiking, rock climbing, white-water rafting.

These guys helped teach me that, if you invest yourself in the people around you, you can find an endless supply of rich relationships. And I expect that many of those friendships I developed during my last two years at Taylor will last my whole lifetime—with guys like Johnny A, Block, Player, Seah Waga, Tall Bob, Big Dave, Sweet Phil, Hat, AP, G, Fish, Crazy, Crosswalk, Turbo, Hot Tub, Big T, Mitch, Drewski, and Lucky Number 7. ("First Berg" was big on nicknames.)

A growing contentment with my relationships translated into a better feeling about my entire college experience. Though I never became an academic star, my grades remained acceptable.

I can't claim to have had a deep sense of calling or a clear and certain vision of the future in terms of a career. I decided part of my struggle over a major the first couple of years was my resistance to being boxed in. I'd known that feeling too often in my life—which could be why I now felt comfortable about majoring in communications. It left me any number of directions to go, while setting no limits on my potential.

Sure, sales and public relations seemed like good possibilities. I'd spent a lifetime selling myself and perfecting my public relation skills.

I even joked about being the perfect morning talk-show host. I wouldn't even have to say anything. They could just zoom the camera in on me, and I could sit there and smile. That would certainly wake people up. And it could also cure anyone who got out of bed grumpy. One look at me, and they'd be thinking, *Maybe my problems aren't so bad after all.*

Chapter 22

College life couldn't have gone much better for me my last two years. After the *Public Eye* pieces aired, one of the top executives of a California company called Electronic Arts phoned to say he'd been very impressed by all that he'd seen and heard about me. So I decided it couldn't hurt to apply for a summer internship with the company. So that's how I came to spend the summer between my junior and senior years working in the beautiful San Francisco Bay area of California, doing PR, testing products, and getting paid to play video games for, would you believe it, EA Sports. It was one of those "it's a tough job but somebody's got to do it" things.

When I'd phone home at night and tell my dad about testing the new features on the latest version of some baseball game that wasn't going to reach the stores for months, he'd laugh at the notion of his son, the video game fanatic, getting paid to play video games. Who would have believed it? Certainly not Dad, who'd often seen me playing with friends and said, "You can't earn a living playing video games, Joel." Now I was proving him wrong.

But I couldn't believe it either. I had to pinch myself almost every day. If someone had asked me, "If you could get a job doing anything in the world, what would it be?" I probably would have said, "Playing video games."

May as well dream big. Because dreams can come true.

Truth is, I didn't just get to play video games starring big-time athletes, the company arranged for me to meet face-to-face a number of athletes featured in those games. One day when the Chicago Cubs were in town, I went out to Candlestick Park, hung around on the field during batting practice, and then went into the locker room to talk with guys like Barry Bonds, Sammy Sosa, and

Giants' manager at the time, Dusty Baker. The Giants not only gave me luxury box seats for the game; they sent me home with all the autographed balls, hats, jerseys and other souvenirs I could carry.

What a life! And what a blast I had doing that internship. But at the end of the summer, when my boss at EA Sports talked about job opportunities after my graduation from college, I knew I had some serious thinking and praying to do about my future.

For while I like to have fun, at school I was learning that the greatest fun is enjoying myself and bringing glory to God at the same time. While I could do that at EA Sports, I also felt that God was calling me to do something different from the ordinary—something besides a nine-to-five job. As I told the reporter from a San Francisco television station who did a feature on me while I was out there, "My ministry can be anywhere. I get attention wherever I am, so I can have an impact on people, and God can have an impact on people through me. Anywhere. Everywhere."

> *"My ministry can be anywhere. I get attention wherever I am, so I can have an impact on people, and God can have an impact on people through me. Anywhere. Everywhere."*

Because I believed that, I continued to accept opportunities to share my story and exercise my leadership skills on and off campus during the rest of my time at Taylor. I spoke to a group of doctors, nurses, and other emergency medical experts at the Rural Trauma Symposium in Portland, Indiana. I spoke at a large church in Ann Arbor, Michigan, and was a keynote speaker at both the Indiana Firefighters Ball down in Indianapolis and at an international Campus Crusade convention out in Colorado. CBS Television's Dan Rather updated the *Public Eye* coverage by retelling my story in a broadcast of *48 Hours* in the summer of 1999. There were feature stories about me in *Indianapolis Monthly*, *Campus Life* magazine, and *The Christian Reader*. My fellow students elected me vice president of my senior class, and the governor of Indiana presented me with a "Distinguished Hoosier" award. But the honor I was most proud of was when the students at Taylor University voted me to receive the annual John Wengatz Award for spiritual leadership on campus.

Yet, despite all these honors and opportunities, I went into the final semester of my college experience with no more certainty about the future than I'd had when I arrived at Taylor the fall of my freshman year. As strange as it may sound, my time at EA Sports had been a real turning point in my personal searching process. During and after that "dream" internship, I really wrestled with the question of my future career and how God would have me use the gifts he had given me. While there would be nothing wrong with wanting to work at Electronic Arts (an option that very much appealed to me), I didn't feel called to be behind a desk all day—at least not yet.

But my own conviction that God had a definite plan for my future and the encouragement of others who assured me of that (including my parents and Jay Kesler) weren't always easy to remember. Especially in the wake of one experience I had just weeks before graduation.

One of my roommates in my senior year, John Aoun, was from France. From the time we met as freshmen, we'd talked about visiting his home in Paris. But it wasn't until spring break of our senior year that we finally pulled off the plan. John and I and a half dozen other friends from Bergwall were going to spend our last spring break together in Paris!

We booked the cheapest international flights we could find out of a major U.S. city. And since a couple of us had friends at another college near our point of departure, my buddies and I decided to pay a visit to that campus on our way to the airport.

Wouldn't you know it, we showed up at this school on a weekend when the entire campus was abuzz with plans and activities surrounding some big annual open house-type event in which all dorms participated. There were lavish decorations in every lounge and every hall. Many of the people we saw were *very* dressed up and decked out. And a number of others had donned a variety of costumes.

As soon as I saw what was going on, I should have anticipated trouble, what with my history with Halloween. But this was springtime. We knew nothing about this event ahead of time, and we were planning to be there just long enough to say hello to a couple of friends.

While our buddy headed upstairs in one of the dorms to look for his friend's room, my other friends and I hung out in a wildly decorated, black-lit lobby, examining the surroundings and watching passersby. Being as attuned as I am to other people's reactions, I overheard some of the students walking past say things like "Did you see that?" and "That's just sick."

Yet I didn't think they meant to be offensive. The way they'd looked right at me, I sensed there was something else going on. But I was pretty sure none of my buddies even noticed. So I said to my roommate, "Johnny, I think some of the people here think I'm wearing a mask." He looked at me kinda funny, like he didn't know what I was talking about. So I let it drop.

But since I knew what I'd heard, I took a seat farther out of the traffic pattern and tried to sink out of sight. A few minutes later a guy approached me. He stopped right in front of my chair and said, "That's the most disgusting costume I've ever seen."

All my buddies froze. They were shocked. They didn't know what to do or say. I was feeling the judgment of this guy in front of me and the pressure from my friends all around me to do something. So I tried to defuse the situation and play along. I smiled and said, "Thanks a lot!"

I knew if he realized the truth, he might have this on his conscience for life. And he didn't deserve that. If I thought he was just being rude, I could have made him feel like dirt. But this was an honest mistake, and I was going to try to let it go.

Peering closer at me in the dim light, he took a step forward and said, "Don't I know you from somewhere?"

I shrugged. "I don't know. Do you? Possibly."

Dead silence. My buddies' jaws had dropped to the floor. You could feel the tension building in the room.

The guy just stood there. Staring at me. Then he said, "I don't know. Say something again."

I repeated what I'd just said. "I don't know. Do you?"

And the guy shook his head. "I'm trying to think. You sound so familiar. Who are you?"

I nodded and whispered, "I'll tell you later."

So the guy walked out. Then my friends and I cracked up, knowing we'd never see him again.

I shrugged it off as just a case of me being in the wrong place at the wrong time. The guy didn't mean to be unkind. He and the others who'd made comments thought they were passing judgment on my taste in horror costumes. He would have been terribly embarrassed, maybe even emotionally devastated, to realize that he was commenting on my everyday appearance.

But the fact that this incident took place on another college campus made me wonder, *Is the real world always going to be like this? Will it ever change?*

I wanted to believe that it could.

And long before graduation time arrived, I managed to put that experience behind me and began to focus again on my hopes for the future. So when my fellow classmates elected me to be the student representative to speak at commencement, I had no trouble preparing remarks that would be honestly optimistic and upbeat.

Sitting on the platform with all the dignitaries, looking out over a packed auditorium on a sweltering late-May afternoon, I couldn't help but compare this scene to my similar experience during freshman orientation. This time I'd had weeks rather than minutes to decide what to say, but I wasn't sure the added time helped relieve much of the pressure I was feeling. The students sitting in front of me this time were no longer strangers. The years we'd spent together on the campus of Taylor University in the tiny, nowhere town of Upland, Indiana, had bonded us together in countless interwoven relationships that would never end. We'd been strangers when we arrived at freshman orientation. Now we were friends. More than friends. We were family. My Taylor family.

What do you say to a family about to part—knowing you'll never all be together again? I'd never been a college graduate before! What wisdom did I have to share that could help these friends and family, who'd meant so much to me, through the transition that lay ahead for all of us?

Early in the program, when my turn came to speak, I stepped to the microphone and scanned the auditorium. I took a quick mental note of my graduating friends, and then my family, which on that day included Betty Dew, my intensive care nurse from Shriners Hospital in Boston, who'd traveled to Upland to be with me and my family for the first time in almost twenty years. I took a deep breath and formally addressed my audience:

Chairman Robbins, members of the Board of Trustees, President Kesler, faculty, classmates, family, and friends, I have found one more use for duct tape. People with small bald heads can't keep caps on very well.

[To demonstrate, I stepped to the side of the podium so everyone could see and doubled over at the waist. When they saw that my mortarboard remained firmly fixed to my noggin, the entire auditorium exploded in laughter and applause. I stepped back to the microphone.]

I had some buddies from First Berg slap some on there so it won't come off.

[I paused until the final titter of laughter subsided. Then I began with what I really wanted to say.]

I had a dream when I was younger. I always wanted to be a talented musician. I always wanted to play a musical instrument of some kind. My mom toured with an international singing group, and my dad played the trumpet. So I figured I should have some rhythm, right?

In sixth grade I decided to tap into my hidden talents. I joined the band. I was a drummer. A drummer with one stick. Now I could have taped a stick to my left arm, but that wasn't me. Later I thought maybe I could play the trumpet instead. It only has three buttons that you need to push. Then I realized you needed lips to play the trumpet.

Believing that God was leading me somewhere else, the next year I joined the middle school choir. That lasted for two years—until puberty hit, and my voice changed. Knowing that the Lord could perform any miracle I asked for, I remember praying, *God, please, please help me play one instrument well.* To this day I can easily count the number of instruments I am capable of playing well. Let's see, there's the tambourine. And the ever so romantic triangle.

One time in chapel I saw the weirdest instrument. It had one long string coming out of a drum. All the musician had to do was pluck that one string. I remember nudging the guy sitting next to me. "Dude, I can play that!" He looked at me strange and went, "Ooo-kay."

It wasn't until my sophomore year here at Taylor that I realized what instrument it was that God had given me to play. I went to a hospital clinic in Cincinnati, and there, during my routine checkup, a nurse asked me to take part in one of their research projects. I agreed. So they hooked me up to a machine and gave me breathing exercises. The results from those exercises were off the charts. My lung capacity scores were 200 to 300 percent. Now if that was on a grading scale of 4.0, my GPA would be 8.0 or 12.0.

After searching all this time, I finally discovered which instrument was mine to play. My instrument is my voice. I shouldn't even have a voice. If you've ever spent much time around people who are burned, you know this is the case. Many have severe lung problems from smoke inhalation. They talk with raspy voices because their lungs are damaged. I don't have lung or vocal chord damage; this is a miracle. . . .

I looked all over to find my dream as a talented musician. I tried to find my dream my own way. But in his own time, the Lord has shown me that my musical talent lies in my voice. And these are my notes.

[I held up the pages I was reading from. A lot of people, including some who had heard me sing, laughed.]

Because of this experience with my dream, I have four things I'd like to share with you today:

Number one: If we belong to God, our dreams are his dreams for us. It would be cruel of God to give a kid with no hands the dream of becoming a drummer—unless he knew there would be a better way. I know he has a dream for me that doesn't require normal hands. For you, he has a dream that uses what you have.

Number two: Don't limit the way that God can fulfill your dreams. The instrument I longed for was preserved for me long before I ever realized it. God may fulfill your dreams differently from what you expect. But it will be no less good.

Number three: Don't be boxed in by your own limitations. I've had limits set for me all my life. When someone told me I couldn't do something, I was more determined to do it. When I think of the future, I'm less worried about my physical limitations than I am about those I've set in my own mind. The boundaries of our own thinking will limit us the most. Let's drop these self-imposed limits.

Number four: Live the dream. In communication classes I studied Martin Luther King's speech, "I Have a Dream." What made his dream special was that he lived it. That's a choice. Not a fate. Outcomes are determined by what we do with our losses. That's our choice. Losing can produce more growth than winning. Let's make up our minds today, classmates, to live the dream. For Jay. For the people who are watching around us. And, most important, for our God.

What are your dreams? Are they right in front of your face, and you don't realize it? Do the limitations of your small worldview sometimes get in the way?

In conclusion, I'd like to read you a poem I wrote. It's short and sweet:

> So dream big dreams;
> nothing is too small.
> Whether you have no fingers at all,
> or all five,
> keep the dream alive.
> Don't just sit around and pray;
> remember the dreams of Jay.
> And when your dreams come true,
> don't forget to give credit where credit is due.

Before I finished the last line of my address, Betty Dew exploded to her feet. Her enthusiastic clapping triggered a thunderous applause that was punctuated with boisterous cheers and piercing whistles. The acclaim went on for so long and was so loud that, even as the volume faded, I imagined it echoing in my mind forever.

A few minutes later, President Kesler handed me my college diploma. And I walked off that stage and into my future, determined to follow my own advice.

Chapter 23

I know my story isn't over. And I can't wait to see where the next chapter takes me. I guess I've always viewed my life in terms of an unusual action-adventure tale. And now that I've shared my adventure through the writing of this book, it seems more of a "story" than ever.

Yet there are two other images that come to mind when I consider my life. Both may be helpful in organizing what I want to say here in closing. The first image is this: over the years I have also come to understand and view my own life as a sort of *magnifying glass*.

Most people who look at me, who glimpse only the outside of my scarred body, usually focus on how different I seem to be from everyone else. The differences are so obvious. However, from the inside looking out, I have slowly come to see in how many ways I am like everyone else. I feel the same universal human emotions. I struggle with the same doubts and insecurities. I face the same relational issues. I've grown up through the same developmental stages and shared most of the same basic life milestones my peers have.

My experience hasn't been so much different as it has just been intensified. Like what happens under a magnifying glass. For example, being human, by definition, means being imperfect. Everyone has flaws. Some of mine are just a lot more obvious than most people's. And perhaps sometimes more difficult to deal with because I can't hide them.

I have slowly come to see in how many ways I am like everyone else. I feel the same universal human emotions. I struggle with the same doubts and insecurities. I face the same relational issues.

Psychologists tell us that everyone longs for acceptance, a sense of belonging, a place to fit in. For me that longing is intensified—and complicated.

At some point in our lives, we all know what it means to suffer. Suffering is just a normal part of the dance of life. Only half-jokingly do I tell people that I think everyone should have to check into a hospital for surgery once a year; there would be many valuable lessons learned about dependency, mortality, and humility. We'd all have a different perspective on life.

All human beings fail and experience serious losses at some point in life. I've lost more than enough to realize that losing can teach us more than winning does.

Most people would acknowledge the importance of setting priorities in life and admit they ought to carefully consider the consequences of their actions and then be more deliberate in what they do, in where they go and when. My life forces me to do that. I can't make a decision to go to Wal-Mart without asking myself, *How badly do I need to go? Is it worth facing the stares and then standing in line behind some woman holding a little kid who will turn around, spot me, and start screaming in terror?* The consequences of even the simplest decisions are often complicated and magnified for me.

The greatest insecurities in life stem from feeling unlovable or unacceptable—and everyone deals with those issues at some time or other. I've had more reason to wonder and worry about that than most people do.

Thankfully, my parents really came through for me on that score. In part because they recognized my intensified need for it, they provided me an incredible sense of sacrificial love and acceptance. That provided the foundation of hope I needed in order to believe that other people might accept me. But most important of all, their example enabled me to believe that God, as my perfect heavenly parent, could accept and love me even more.

Many basic human emotions have been intensified for me—anger, for example. Psychology 101 teaches that anger is the natural human response to pain, fear, or frustration. I've experienced lots of all three—so I've had to learn to deal with anger.

My list of common life issues that have been magnified in my personal experience could go on and on. I'll mention just one more here. My search for a healthy self-identity and an accurate self-awareness has sometimes seemed like an epic quest because of my circumstances. When you appear more alien than human, there's a different twist, a little deeper significance, to the universal human questions "Who am I?" and "Where do I fit into this world?"

It's easy—too easy, too simplistic, in fact—to just say, "Be yourself!" You gotta find yourself first. A lot of people asking "Who am I?" end up taking their cues—good and bad—from how others see them. For me that wasn't so easy. Other people never see us quite the way we see ourselves. Here again, that's even more true for me.

I still don't like to look in a mirror because the image I see looking back at me is not the complete picture I have of myself. So who's to say what that right image is?

Actually, I've learned that God's Word acts as the best possible mirror for me. When I study the Bible, I see myself as I relate to God. The Bible focuses not on the surface but on the spirit inside. (I love that encouraging verse [1 Samuel 16:7] that tells me, "Man looks at the outward appearance, but the LORD looks at the heart.") Scripture also provides me with a crystal clear picture of what I should look like, who I should be modeling myself after, and what I should be working toward.

The second image I think of as I review my life is a little harder to convey than that of a magnifying glass. I'll have to introduce it the way I first heard it—by paraphrasing a story, or maybe it was a sermon illustration, attributed to my neighbor Billy Graham:

 One very ordinary afternoon a young boy was walking home from school by his usual route. The worn dirt path he always followed ran alongside a farmer's field of corn. This unremarkable cornfield was bordered by an ordinary woven-wire fence. Suddenly, up ahead, on one of the fence posts between the cornfield and the path this young boy saw a very startling sight.

There, the bottom of his shell resting firmly on the top of that fence post, was a big box turtle, furiously kicking all four feet like he was swimming in the air. The boy couldn't help laughing out loud before he asked the turtle, "And how in the world did you get up there?"

Even before he posed the question, the boy knew the answer. It was all too obvious. Despite the impressive way the turtle now flailed his legs, he had not managed to fly to the top of the fence post; he could never have managed to jump that high. Nor could any turtle have climbed straight up that fence post and balanced himself so nicely on top. There was only one possible explanation for such a strange and unexpected phenomenon. Someone had found that creature turtling along on the ground, picked him up, and deliberately placed him there.

I share that story because, at this time in my life, I relate to that image. I am a lot like a *turtle on a fence post*. The point being this: I've plodded this far through life. Now I find myself on a very visible platform. I seem to be making little or no progress on my own. I'm not always sure what I'm doing here or what's going to happen next. But one thing is obvious: just like that turtle, I didn't get where I am today by myself.

My parents, my family, school teachers and administrators, friends like Ryan, and medical professionals at Shriners and elsewhere have picked me up and brought me a long way. I certainly wouldn't be here without them. But I have no doubt that it was God—whose sovereignty, omnipotence, wisdom, and creativity (no doubt bolstered by a great sense of humor) are unequaled—who carefully placed me right where I am. Like that turtle on the fence post, I've been given a remarkable and unexpected platform.

Not only has God blessed me with life itself, he's also given me a very, very special gift in the form of my disability.

How do I know that God is the one who has done this? Because he also has given me the gifts I have needed to get here, and the gifts I will need to make the most of this unusual platform.

Not only has God blessed me with life itself, plus all the ordinary yet wonderful gifts he designed for all human beings—family, intelligence, language, the capacity for fellowship (with him and with others), and so much more; he's also given me a very, very special gift in the form of my disability.

I don't say this lightly. I certainly don't want to be trite. But I have come to view my disability as an incredibly valuable gift. Let me give you just a few reasons.

First of all, my disability acts as an extremely effective filter in all my relationships. The very first time I meet someone, that person's initial reaction to me tells me worlds about them—what they think, how they relate to others, and who they really are.

Also, living a lifetime with my disability has fine-tuned my senses to the point that I'm hyperaware of everyone and of everything going on around me. I pick up on even the most subtle changes of expression; I'm great at reading body language. That, too, has taught me to be a pretty good and quick judge of people.

My experience makes it easy to notice and empathize with other hurting people. Perhaps that's the reason, along with my own obvious vulnerability, why I'm constantly surprised by how many people quickly open up and express to me their deepest feelings and problems.

My disability is also a gift in that it has made me a very memorable person. People who meet me never seem to forget the experience. They might not remember my name, but, I guarantee you, they remember the face. Being so memorable means I have the potential to make an ongoing difference in the lives of everyone I meet. Knowing I won't be forgotten means my actions and my words matter. What I do, what I say when I meet and spend time with someone, will have a more lasting impact because our encounter will be remembered. These are rare gifts I've been given. But I can't appreciate the privilege of possessing them without recognizing the heavy responsibility that comes with it.

It's a uniquely human dream that God has given us to want our existence to better the world by influencing the people and events we encounter in life. In different words it was the last instruction Jesus left for all those who would follow him. Wherever we go, to the uttermost points on earth, we are to search out those people in whose lives we might be able to make a difference. People who would have reason to listen to us. People to whom we could offer more spiritual insight than just spiritual Band-Aids and one-liner fortune cookies. People for whom we might be able to illustrate or exemplify the acceptance, the forgiveness, and the loving provision of a God who cares about each of us more than he cares about anything else in the universe.

Many, if not most, Christians struggle with this assignment. They're uncertain who they should or could reach out to. And when they do, they wonder if their words and their encounters will have any lasting impact—or even be remembered for more than just a day.

That is not my problem.

If I think about it, and I know I should, when I get out of bed every morning, I can be pretty confident that I will impact every single person I meet that day in some way. Good or bad. Some days that's a responsibility I'd rather not bear.

In conclusion, let me tell you about one such time. The encounter took place when my little brother Kyle asked me to come and eat lunch with him and his friends at the same elementary school I'd attended in Black Mountain. Actually, it didn't take place when Kyle first asked because I turned him down that time.

I knew how big a deal it is for grade school kids to have someone—anyone— come and eat lunch with them. And of all the potential guests who might show up, a big brother had to be one of the coolest. Which was why I felt terrible turning Kyle down. I anticipated his disappointment. But still I just said "no!"

You need to understand. For most of my life, young kids have been my least favorite people. Even when I was one, I tried to avoid young children I didn't already know. By the time I approached adulthood, I had mastered the art of avoidance.

I love Kyle dearly. I had diligently prayed for a little brother years before I got one, and, lo and behold, if he didn't turn out to be a little kid. I made a lot of exceptions for him because of who he was, but he did little to change my feelings about young kids in general. They were always unpredictable and often cruel in their response to me—Kyle wasn't, but others were.

Children are also, as a rule, exceedingly persistent. Kyle certainly proved that. No matter how many times I disappointed him by turning down his invitation, he kept asking, "When can you come and eat lunch with me at school, Joel?" Not, *Will you please come and eat lunch with me?* but, *When will you come?*

I put him off time after time, hoping he would consider the consequences; I wanted my brother to really think through the implications of his request. Finally he asked me again, and instead of just saying no, I said, "Kyle, you know what will happen if I go, don't you?"

"What?"

"People are gonna stare. They will make comments. There will be a big scene." I wanted him to know it wouldn't just be a fun time of showing off his big brother.

"I don't care about any of that," Kyle told me. "I just want you to come and eat lunch with me and my friends."

I didn't think it would be that simple. But I'd warned him. So I said, "Okay, Kyle, as long as you know what to expect, I'll do it."

Walking into the cafeteria at Black Mountain Primary School was like step-ping back in time. The same tables with the same chairs—so small that adults had to sit with their knees tucked under their chins. The lunch line with the stainless steel serving tables looked the same as when I was in school. I thought I recognized some of the same cafeteria workers. Definitely the same cardboard pizza. Only this time, they gave me an adult's double serving and two chocolate milks as I went through the line behind Kyle.

We hadn't even found seats yet when it became obvious to me that we were attracting a lot of attention. Everyone in the cafeteria seemed to be whispering and watching where we were going to sit. When I scrunched down in the kiddie chair next to my brother, everyone else at our table seemed to freeze. I wasn't sure Kyle even noticed, so I quickly set out to break the ice by introducing myself to his friends and asking everyone's name.

About the time Kyle's classmates finally seemed to be warming up, I felt this little finger tapping me on the shoulder. I knew what that meant. Some little squirt had worked up the courage—someone may even have dared him—to approach me. Here we go! Slowly I turned around and found myself facing a lit-tle first- or second-grade girl.

"Hi," I said.

She stood there in silence for a few seconds, staring at my face. Then she finally asked, "What happened to you?"

What happened to me? That may be the toughest question of all for me to answer. More difficult even than "Why me, Lord?" or "Why don't you have fin-gers?" Tougher than "What was Reginald Dort thinking?" or even "Did I suffer more than Jesus did on the cross?"

"What happened to you?" is the toughest question I get asked because in my mind it encompasses all those other questions. There is never enough time to answer it adequately. And yet I know how I answer it not only says something about me; it is sometimes the only chance I have to make a positive impression on the person who asked it.

On a deeper level my response to that question can be used as a spiritual barometer; where I am in my walk with the Lord on a given day will not only influ-ence the tone of my answer, but it may determine whether I view the opportunity to respond to the question as an annoyance or a privilege. So I am forced to take a reading of my own spiritual condition every time someone asks, "What happened to you?"

On this particular day, the barometer must have been rising because I smiled at the little girl and said, "A long time ago, when I was just a baby, I was in a car accident. The car caught on fire, and I was burned. When my burns healed, I looked very different on the outside. But on the inside, I'm no different from you and your friends. I have the same kind of feelings you do. I have friends. I like to have fun."

I am forced to take a reading of my own spiritual condition every time someone asks, "What happened to you?"

Almost before I realized it, a dozen kids were standing around, listening for a little bit and then asking questions themselves. "What's your name?" *Joel.* "What happened to your fingers?" *They were burned off in a car accident before I was two years old.* All the kids gasped. "Can you write?" *Sure. See. The doctors built me a new thumb, and it works just fine.* A chorus of "cools" resounded. "What happened to your ears?" *They got burned off in the same accident.* "Can you hear?" *How did you think I was answering these questions?* Everyone laughed.

I heard an endless stream of whats, whys, and how comes before the bell rang that signaled the end of lunch period. The teachers called their charges, and the students lined up with their classmates. I bid good-bye to my brother and his friends, and as I headed out the door of the cafeteria, twenty or more kids were waving and calling, "Bye, Joel!"

As I walked out to my car, reviewing the experience in my mind, the thought hit me: *A year from now I won't remember the name of one of those kids I just met. But chances are, every one of those children I talked to will remember me for the rest of their lives.*

Recalling how I'd always felt about little kids, I could almost picture God looking down and laughing as I realized what an impact I could make with a ministry to children.

Experiences like that often force me to think about the responsibility I feel to use the gifts God has given me. Then I consider the future and can't help wondering, *What does God have for me that I haven't yet received?*

I can hardly wait to find out.

Epilogue

When I look back over my life so far, I don't begin to know why everything happened to me the way it did. But I do know the One who has been with me through it all and has brought me to this point. So even though I don't know exactly where I'm going in life, I do know for whom I'm living.

Because I know who put me on this fence post, because I know who's in control, and because I've seen and appreciate what he's already done, I can trust him with my future. Not that I don't have dreams of my own. I do. But I want my dreams to be the same dreams God has for my life.

I still dream and pray about getting married and having a family someday. I can't wait to have kids with fingers! But I'm content to wait and see how or if God makes provision for that. Some of my dreams are already coming true. I always wanted to write a book, and now I've achieved that dream. Not long ago I finally mastered the art of cracking eggs—which was a pretty significant success in my book. Right up there with when I first managed to open a pop-top soft-drink can. Perhaps I'll learn to tie my own shoes someday.

My dreams come in all sizes. But I remain most concerned about finding a career that I love. Work that not only uses the skills and gifts God has given me but allows me to glorify him at the same time—a job so well suited to me that no one else could do it quite as well.

However I make my living, I dream of having a lifelong speaking ministry. Because I've had so many universal experiences—magnified by my circumstances—I find I have something to say to just about everyone. And I feel that God has specially gifted me to be a communicator at this time in history. We live in a visual age. And I am very much a visual guy.

Even though I dream about the future and anticipate the adventures that lie ahead, I'm learning to be content with where I am on the fence post today. I still struggle some days. Just because I've been through the fire doesn't mean I've been completely purified. God is still working on me.

Just because I've been through the fire doesn't mean I've been completely purified. God is still working on me.

I still get angry sometimes at people's reactions to me. More often, I get frustrated over issues of independence and dependence, which I'm forced to wrestle with a dozen different ways and times on any given day. For example, I grow tired of asking someone to cut up my steak for me. So when I go out to eat, I usually decide what to order based on who's with me or what is not going to require me to cut it up.

When I say I've learned to be content with my disfigurement, I don't mean to be flip or make trite statements such as *Beauty lies within* and *Beauty is only skin-deep*. How I look is who I am. And I'm content with that.

It brings me a real sense of joy when people approach me after they hear me speak, and they say, "When you stand up and start talking, I don't see scars. They just seem to fade away." I understand and appreciate what they are saying. But at the same time, there is part of me that wants to explain, *If you can't see my scars, then you don't really see me. Because those scars are a big part of who I am.*

My story is different. It always has been. That's not gonna change. But it's okay. Because I'll still be me.

Just Joel.

We want to hear from you. Please send your comments about this book to us in care of zreview@zondervan.com. Thank you.

GRAND RAPIDS, MICHIGAN 49530 USA

WWW.ZONDERVAN.COM